I Dare to Open My Suitcase

Johanna Magdalena Griffiths-Britt

To Toni with love

Hanni x

O&U
Onwards & Upwards

Onwards and Upwards Publishers

3 Radfords Turf, Cranbrook, Exeter,
EX5 7DX, United Kingdom
www.onwardsandupwards.org

First edition, published in the United Kingdom by Onwards and Upwards Publishers Ltd. (2019).

ISBN: 978-1-78815-712-4
Typeface: Sabon LT
Graphic design: LM Graphic Design

Author's Note:

To the best of my knowledge all quotations are accurate and true, and every effort has been made to contact copyright holders of quoted books, poems and songs. However, if there are any omissions or inaccuracies, I will make any necessary corrections for future reprints or editions of this book.

Endorsements

Having known Hanni for many years, she has often spoken about putting pen to paper to share her story, and this book is well worth the read. It is a wonderful, true and inspiring story, illustrating her life journey: from her early years feeling lonely and abandoned whilst living in several children's homes in Switzerland; the joy of the 'God-moments' in her life and how she found the Lord; to the emotional and spiritual struggles she faced in caring for her sick husband.

This is an unforgettable story in which we see Hanni grow from an insecure people-pleaser who felt a *nobody*, to a mature Christian who learned to be thankful for all God's blessings and feel a *somebody*. Reading her story brought tears to my eyes, a smile to my face and instilled a wonder that we have such an amazing God. I am sure this book, including scripture verses, poems and reflections, will touch your heart like it did mine.

Chris Ledger
Author, speaker and counsellor

Over many cups of coffee and over a good many years, it has been a privilege to get to know Hanni and learn of her unique and amazing story. General conversation led to and increased in Hanni the desire to write down and share so much of her life with others.

This is a testimony born out of many tears, both of pain and joy. Now we, the readers, can have a glimpse of God's caring, gentle and guiding Hand throughout all the years of Hanni's fruitful life.

Read and be amazed!

Pam Hathorn
Valued friend

Acknowledgements

My first thanks must go to the Lord God of the Bible.

Thanks also to...

- My dear friend Wendy, who voluntarily and tirelessly sat by me hours on end, persevering alongside me with great love, encouragement and patience as she assisted me in writing my memoirs. I will always have every reason to treasure our time together, which was fun and serious, sombre and bright, tiring and refreshing; thank you, Wendy!
- Pam and Carolyn, who in the very first place listened to my story and encouraged me enormously to start writing about my "life as it was"!
- Maureen and John, who always included me and my family into their own family life.
- Angela and Graham, who regularly, and for years, shared their caring hospitality.

Further, I have been given so many amazing, wonderful and meaningful friends, and every name noted here on this paper made a true impact on my life. I am eternally thankful for having known you all, especially...

- Liz, Jim and family; Ann and Malcolm; Ann and Paul; Kathy, Mars and family; Britt; Karen; Sophia, Mick and family; Bunny and Barry; Geraldine; Judith; Kathy; Janet; Karen; Gill and Keith.
- Deirdre, Graham and family; Anna; Sandra; Pauline; Malcolm and Cathy; Deborah and all of the Greyfriars church, especially the 'Time Out for Women' group. Thank you!

Thanks to all of my late husband's family.

Thanks also to my Swiss family and friends:

- Anni and Rolf, my longest friends in Christ who faithfully, year after year, provided hospitality every time I needed it and further helped by taking care of my mother's needs when I moved to the UK.
- Elisabeth and Hansjurg; I thank you for always being willing to translate from German to English.

A wholehearted 'thank you' to my second cousin, Marcel Britt, who voluntarily did all the graphic design for a previous self-published edition of my book.

Thanks to my Malaysian nursing colleagues. My fondness goes to all of you for enhancing my life through rich and steadfast friendships; without you my life would not have been the same. Thank you!

And so I could go on with my thanksgiving as different names tumble forth from my memory bank of past and present friends who lovingly supported me. You know who you are; I thank you and do not forget that we together are part of this ongoing story... and that God has not yet finished with us!

About the Author

Born in Switzerland as an only child to a single mother, Hanni had an isolated upbringing living for seventeen years in children's homes. Her passionate desire to become a person in her own right was fuelled by the immense emotional and intellectual struggles of her early years. At eighteen she committed her life to Jesus Christ, and later qualified as a nurse in Switzerland. After moving to England, which has become her 'home', Hanni trained in midwifery and gained UK Citizenship as well as getting married at age thirty-eight. Hanni is now a widow and has one married daughter and three grandchildren who live in Switzerland.

To my daughter
Helen,

my son in law
Roman,

my grandchildren
Anna, Evan and Sophie,

my late husband
George Herbert Desmond Griffiths

and all those that choose to enjoy reading my story.

Contents

Note to Reader

For ease of reading, please note that each letter has the following layout:

- Title of the letter
- A quote
- The letter
- Reflection

These have been gathered from my past diaries which include quotes, Bible verses, Bible studies, illustrations, prayers and words of songs. These entries and records have together enabled me to identify and express meaning in the comings and goings of my life and thus have often acted as stepping stones. By stepping stones, I mean to say that they have taken me from one place of experience to another, providing insight as to how to live my life.

And so I decided that each letter would include what I call 'reflections', which I have picked out from my journals to place at the end of each letter. These are treasures of my life's story and my desire to pass them on is my joy. Although these reflections are there to enhance the content of the letter, they can also be read independently on other occasions.

Introduction

Why am I telling my story? To answer this question, we need to look back to when I was fourteen years old, cooped up with twenty-five other girls in a children's home in the east of Switzerland. We all had different reasons for being at the home. For me, my mother had become pregnant as an unmarried woman, which led to her being cast out from her family. At the time, as there was no provision for her to care for me, I was taken into care at ten days old. Although the father was completely absent from my life, I do refer to him in my story.

Could anything good come out of my life? I was preoccupied with this question for many years, especially when, aged seventeen, it was time for me to leave the children's home.

My avid journal-keeping, which I kept up for many years, has been a great help in piecing together my life's story. I share these memoirs in this book thematically rather than chronologically. By telling my story, I hope to open a window on my experience of how the God of the Bible influenced my life, taking me from what felt like a sense of emptiness to being filled with a glorious sense of purpose of the meaning of life.

And it is my desire for you, the reader, to understand and believe that none of us need to be victims of our past. None of us, as I have learned from my own experience, need to carry all our emotional baggage and unresolved memories, and the inevitable feeling of painful isolation.

So you will see in this book that I dared to open the suitcase of my life, look at my baggage and gradually unpack and resolve what needs to stay and what needs to go! At other times, items fell out, interrupting and challenging my way of life. Therefore, this book contains reflections of my personal story and describes how I was turned inside out but also how I was restored to a new being for good and wholeness by the grace of God.

It is not so much *my* story that you are hearing but a story of old, a story of restoration which I too experienced as I journeyed through my life. The Bible says:

For we are God's handiwork, created in Christ Jesus to do good works, which God prepared in advanced for us to do.

Ephesians 2:10

From this I believe that my story is for sharing, and encouragement that there is a way to live a healthy, intelligent and meaningful life. Although the process of my restoration has been slow, from where I stand, in my eighties, I can see it was all worth it as I feel so rich in my faith of Christ Jesus. Of course, I will still go on learning to live as God has planned until the day when my earthly life will come to an end.

Finally, dear reader, let me reiterate that my ultimate desire is that you will be inspired as you read these pages to live your life as God intended for you.

So I want to begin with a piece which partly portrays a picture of my life as being a 'chosen vessel of God' and which reflects some aspects of what I have written in the pages of this book.

The Chosen Vessel

The master was searching for a vessel to use;
Before him were many,
Which one would he choose?

"Take me," cried the gold one,
"I'm shiny and bright,
I'm of great value and I do things just right.

My beauty and lustre will outshine the rest,
And for someone like you, Master,
Gold would be best."

The Master passed on with no word at all,
And looked at a silver urn narrow and tall,
"I'll serve you, dear Master, I'll pour out your wine,
I'll be on your table whenever you dine.
My lines are so graceful,
My carvings so true,
And silver will always compliment you."

Unheeding, the Master passed on to the brass,
Wide-mouthed and shallow and polished like glass.
"Here! Here!" cried the vessel, "I know I will do,
Place me on your table for all men to view."

"Look at me," called the goblet of crystal so clear,
"My transparency shows my contents so dear.
Though fragile am I, I will serve you with pride,
And I'm sure I'll be happy in your house to abide."

The Master came next to a vessel of wood,
Polished and carved, it solidly stood.
"You may use me, dear Master,"

The wooden bowl said,
"But I'd rather you used me for fruit, not for bread."

Then the Master looked down and saw a vessel of clay,
Empty and broken it helplessly lay.
No hope had the vessel
That the Master might choose
To cleanse, and make whole, to fill, and to use.

"Ah! This is the vessel I've been hoping to find,
I'll mend it and use it and make it mine.
I need not the vessel with pride of itself,
Nor one that is narrow to sit on the shelf,
Nor one that is big-mouthed and shallow and loud,
Nor one that displays his contents so proud,
Not the one that thinks he can do all things right,
But this plain, earthly vessel, filled with power and might."

Then gently he lifted the vessel of clay,
Mended and cleansed it, and filled it that day;
Spoke to it kindly – "There's work you must do –
Just pour out to others, as I pour into you."

Beulah V. Cornwall (1901-1981)

LETTER 1

"Commit to the Lord
whatever you do,
and your plans will
succeed.
In his heart a man
plans his course,
but the Lord
determines his steps."

Proverbs 16:3,9

Highlight of My Life – Your Birth

How did I meet your dad?

My dear daughter Helen,

Just as a painter paints a picture, so am I starting today not to paint on a canvas but to paint a picture of my life through writing letters to you. And of course, I will start on a blank canvas, as it were, gradually bringing together various strands of what has made and is making up my life, thus hoping to give you an insight into my history of how and why I came to be the person I am today.

So for a starter I will give you a sketch of my life that started in two different children's homes. I knew nothing else than growing up and being educated within the walls of these homes, sharing my life exclusively with likeminded girls, ages ranging from seven to seventeen years old. As a consequence, I became accustomed to believing that my birth was an accident due to the fact that I did not seem to belong to a particular family. Looking back, I was labelled an orphan, and later on in my life I heard another nametag: "illegitimate"! To be an illegitimate child in those days was a description that society frowned upon, making me feel less valued. Yes, I do remember as I grew up that I used to feel isolated and different from everybody else, hence developing characteristics that later caused me problems of one kind or another. I will write to you about these things in future letters.

After the birth, my mother needed help with my care. I have no idea how we landed under the care of the Salvation Army, but I gathered that they picked my mother up at the end of her pregnancy and placed me, ten days after my birth, in a cot in one of their homes. Related to this time, I was given a photograph of those very early days which showed that in the same room were ten more cots with babies and each child tucked up in its blanket looking exactly the same. No wonder that we were labelled individually with our name for identification. And what name they would have written at the head of my cot, I don't know, since Johanna Magdalena, I feel, would have been a rather adult name for a baby.

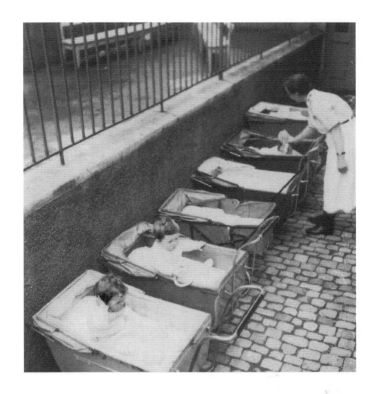

And you know, regarding this photo... I used to often look at this picture; I treasured it as it provided me with some kind of comfort that I was not the only child who had to learn to accept a different way of growing up and being family. It also provided me with an understanding and acceptance that society was not just made up of functional families but also with lots of children living together cared for by 'nice' people. And considering my situation, the children's home certainly provided me with a safe place to live, grow and develop, for which I am truly thankful. Mind you, at the same time, my thinking sometimes went in a different direction – I considered another label that might have been given to me, for example a 'no-one wants you' child. I used to liken this label to a plant that had no prospect of flowering and therefore was suited only for natural waste on a compost heap, because my sense of self-worth was extremely low. Regarding this feeling of being 'no use for anything', I am going to reflect on and write about how a 'nobody' or a 'non-significant infant' came to be transformed to someone of self-worth and self-respect.

So there was literally a time in my life when I believed that I had no chance to progress to a normal and better life, which therefore led me to the symbolism of a dead plant fit only for the compost. But I learned – ha, ha, ha! – that to be composted had its use too. And what do I mean by being composted? Well, you most likely know that the rotting down of natural waste takes place with heat, light, darkness and air and will eventually turn the material into nourishment, furthering new and healthy life somewhere else in the garden. This sort of process takes time and effort but makes good use of unwanted material and, in the end, it will definitely cultivate and strengthen new growth in the natural world. And so, for me, this kind of 'compost development' spells out the old being replaced by the new, which, I feel, is a powerful metaphor describing something that has taken place in my life. Through my letters, I intend to reveal this process, with my themes focusing on:

- how my upbringing influenced my developing thought-world;
- how my character and my views of others changed;
- how I became in dire need for the old to be transformed into the new;
- thus, how the 'old' material provided nourishment for the wilting side of the plant and, of course, metaphorically the plant being me!

And so in this moment, my heart rejoices at the prospect of unveiling all this because the 'God of Heaven' has been good to me: allowing this transformation to take place; lifting me to my potential and being so instrumental by speaking biblical truth into my life; turning me, so to speak, inside-out and upside-down, reshaping my nothingness to a beautiful flower. Awesome! And the following words of an old song spring to mind:

> *How great is our God? How great is his name?*
> *He is the greatest one, forever the same.*
> *He rolled back the waters of the mighty Red Sea and said,*
> *I'll never leave you; put your trust in me.*

"Put your trust in me" has become one of my life's mottos because I have confidence in the reliability of my Creator God and, as you know, I do trust him with my life. Permit me now to move on and give you a brief outline of my practical life. My personal diary is useful as I look back on those days; I am very grateful that I did not throw the pages out as they truly provide memories which I might well have forgotten. And I know full well that recording things gives me a better chance to remember, to consider and to recapture the various events of my life. I am also aware that my story may be similar to another's – and yet in my heart I know that it is unique.

I will now skip ahead in my story. I trained as a nurse in Basle, Switzerland in 1958-1961 and worked there as a staff nurse for two years. Thereafter I journeyed to England in June 1963 to take up a job as a nurse auxiliary in Bromley Kent in order to learn the English language with the hope of later working as a qualified nurse. And sure enough, in November 1963 I received the official papers stating my English qualification as a State Registered Nurse (SRN). In other words, The General Nursing Council of England and Wales acknowledged and accepted my Swiss Nursing Training as being of equal standard.

What is more, through my profession I was given the opportunity to meet your dad. So let me tell you how this meeting took place and led to our marriage.

On one of my working days he arrived on my ward as a patient for a minor operation. After being introduced to him as the sister in charge of the ward, he looked at me with a large grin on his face exclaiming, "I have met you before!" But as for me, I had totally forgotten the incident of our first meeting and he kindly jogged my memory of six months earlier when he had given me and a colleague a lift from Richmond to Ealing where we all lived. He remembered me for my accent, face and the unusual circumstances under which we had met: when my colleague and I asked him to point us to the bus stop to return to Ealing, he himself drove us back to our homes.

I had the pleasure of looking after him for a few days before he was discharged, which for me was the end of this encounter – but not for him. He started to call regularly at my workplace with a bunch of flowers accompanied by his big smile. As he was not a big talker and obviously could not stay long, I felt that he was trying to say something with his regular visits and the bringing of flowers. I do remember well his big beaming smile showing his white teeth which was part of what I was impressed by and attracted to. Hence, this continuous 'getting to know you' went on for a number of months. All my colleagues watched with interest, and as we both were very shy, the courtship was extremely slow. I eventually discovered that he had a commitment to his elderly father who lived with him and therefore nothing could be rushed. But to the surprise of us all, the father suddenly died, which gave way for our friendship to progress more quickly. I was then introduced to his two sisters and their families and in due time he asked me to marry him at Christmas of that year.

Our wedding took place in Ealing on 27th June 1974, celebrating with his family, his friends from work, my friends from the hospital, the principal of the Bible College, and a tutor who had stood by me ever since I attended their two-year Christian Training Course. Switzerland was represented by my mother and a friend who had been in the same Salvation Army's children home. It truly turned out to be a great and memorable day. Getting married to your father was an absolute plus as he was able to bring in some stability to my otherwise fragmented life – and for the first time I had a real family.

The next sketch on my writing canvas is of the good news a year later when you were born. What an amazing wonder and experience that all was, my dear Helen!

Let me recall the time of my nine months of pregnancy including when I discovered that not everything had gone according to plan. I proudly admit that my midwifery training became very useful as I was familiar with the impending changes that were to take place as you grew within my body. However, at week fifteen I discovered an unusual swelling on the left side at the end of my tummy, and so for the next three weeks I kept an eye on the lump, wondering whether it was part of my baby or something more sinister. After my own regular examinations of the area I realised that the lump was growing bigger and sensed that there might be something wrong. Sure enough, the doctor was not pleased with what she felt and saw. Immediately, I was sent to the Hammersmith Hospital and the very next day a surgeon performed a laparotomy in which he discovered that I had a pear-shaped lump attached to the outside of my womb which, if left, would have grown bigger, taking space away from you growing inside me.

You can well imagine, can't you, how we felt after hearing this report? Discouragement was huge because we were told that we might lose our child, which would have been a devastating experience. The word went around to many of my friends from different parts of the world, who set about praying earnestly for you to be allowed to stay put and grow to full gestation, and sure enough, you did. Praise God! After some days in hospital, I returned home with continuous close supervision by my paediatrician, who was a committed Christian. And so the time arrived when you were born in the afternoon on 6th October 1975. It all happened like this:

My waters broke in the middle of the night. I continued to be in labour for many hours but not making satisfactory progress, therefore the decision was taken by the same Christian doctor to perform an emergency Caesarean section at four o'clock in the afternoon. *Wonderful* – you, Helen Winifred, our precious daughter, were born at 4.28pm, weighing 3.560 kg. What an incredible event your birth was to us all. You looked spotless: no wrinkles, lovely long dark hair and a full round face. Your dad saw you before I did, and he was bowled over by your absolutely perfect appearance.

Considering the disturbance we had experienced during the pregnancy, we both were deeply convinced that your birth was nothing short of a miracle and we felt such an honour and privilege to be trusted by the Creator God to become a mother and father to our baby girl.

Amazing! I was so full of joy, and these words fell out of my mouth: "I praise you, Lord, for this most precious gift of life. I thank you for the wonder of new life displayed in our daughter. And I pray that you would give us grace to look after your gift in a responsible way: showering meaningful love; cherishing what we have received; and bringing our daughter up as best as we know how. I ask that we as parents may be a continuous blessing in her life, and in advance, I thank you that she in turn will be a blessing to us. Amen!"

I also added the following words that mirror the priestly blessing spoken of in the Old Testament:

"The Lord bless you, Helen, and keep you; the Lord make his face to shine upon you and be gracious to you; the Lord turn his face towards you and give you peace."[1]

I had learned that in ancient history Moses gave these words of blessing to his brother Aaron and to Aaron's sons because God commanded, and hence it became the tradition that the priests blessed the Hebrew people every morning after the sacrifice made at the temple. In addition, I had learned that today many synagogues end their service with this blessing and that this has even filtered down and is being used in our Christian services.

I, for one, have always loved the meaning of these ageless words and believed it to be the right time and occasion to declare this blessing of God into your life.

And so, my lovely, incredible, precious daughter, I close this letter affirming that I shall always be so thankful and proud of you,

Mum

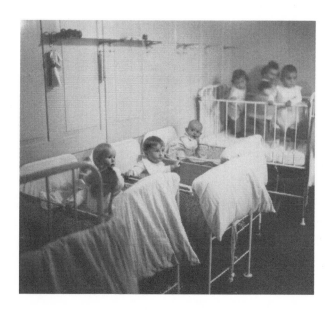

---

[1] cp. Numbers 6:24-26

Reflection

Look at the birds of the air; they do not sow or reap or store away in barns, and yet your heavenly Father feeds them. Are you not much more valuable than they?

Matthew 6:26

Hearing Jesus speaking these words into my life is hard to comprehend as I have a tendency to believe that I am of no value because of the messages I absorbed in the past and that influenced my view of myself. Thus, to discover that Jesus thinks differently is something I want to hang on to, rather than to the feelings of my past.

I learned the following song from an American Gospel singer at the Billy Graham Crusade at Earls Court in London where I sang in the choir in the seventies:

Why should I feel discouraged and why should the shadow fall?
Why should my heart be lonely and long for heaven and home?
When Jesus is my portion, a constant friend is he,
His eye is on the sparrow and I know he watches me.
I sing because I am happy; I sing because I am free,
His eye is on the sparrow and I know he watches me.

"Counting your blessings and sharing it with others makes countless happiness in life" is a saying that seems to be good advice and reminds me of another song called *Count Your Blessings*, written by Johnson Oatman (1897), which undoubtedly has influenced my attitude to put being thankful into practice whether I feel like it or not:

Count your blessings, name them one by one,
Count your blessings, see what God has done!
Count your blessings, name them one by one,
And it will surprise you what the Lord has done.

W. J. DANIEL & CO. LTD.

DEPARTMENT STORE

NEWBURY, WINDSOR, EALING, LONDON, W.13
ASSOCIATE COMPANY, READING

TELEPHONE: EALING 6789

96/108, Uxbridge Road
West Ealing
W. 13

VAT 226 7049 63.

Mr. Griffiths,
107, Coldershaw Road,
W. 13.   July 2nd. 1974.

RESTAURANT

Wedding reception held on June 29th. 1974.

70 lunches @ £2.70. each.	£	189. 00.
45 sherry's @ 22p.		9. 90.
12 bottles Asti		28. 80.
16 Orange Squashes		1. 92.
	£	229. 62.
Service charge		22. 96.
	£	252. 58.
Hire of room		20. 00.
Hire of Cakestand & knife		2. 05.
	£	274. 63.
Cigerettes		36
	£	274. 99.
VAT 10%		27. 49.
Bar expenses		33. 17.
	£	335. 65.
Less deposit		30. 00.
	£	305. 65.

Paid by cheque June 29th. 1974.

W. J. Daniel & Co. Ltd.,

PAID
WITH THANKS

LETTER 2

"You know me inside and out,
you know every bone in my body;
You know exactly how I was made, bit by bit,
how I was sculpted from nothing into something.
Like an open book, you watch me grow
from conception to birth;
all the stages of my life were spread out before you.
The days of my life all prepared
before I'd even lived one day."

Psalm 139:14-16 (MSG)

The above verse has had a repeated and profound influence on my developing thoughts, in that I slowly learned to accept the way God my Creator viewed me as being created in his image and for his purpose.

Against All Odds – A Brave Mother-To-Be

One thing only…

Dear daughter,

Let us now look at my mother when she was expecting her child and the subsequent experiences that filled her life with difficulties. Reading the following account will help you to understand why this lady, your grandmother, had to live all her life on the margins of family and society. Her story is depressing but not without hope, so let me explain her life as best as I know how.

Some of the facts and experiences were handed down, of which I am sure I know only a fraction of what occurred during her lifetime. But I know from my mother's records that she was expelled from her own parents' home because of becoming pregnant. Whether the word 'expelled' is too strong, I am not sure, but I am aware that there was a definite rejection over my mother's life by a powerful family figurehead, which would have been my grandmother.

My mother was one of eight children and she was the only child who did not develop physically to a normal height and was seemingly 'mentally backward'. I would rather, from my experience, have described her character as 'simple-minded', shrewd at the right opportunity and totally honest with a humble, happy and contented heart. Nonetheless, I assume that in the days of my grandparents, she was considered an 'abnormal' child and therefore unwanted within the family. It is likely that her mother was ashamed of her own growing child and kept her hidden from family and public life. And this was reflected, too, from the lips of my mother when she expressed some of the emotional pain that she had had to endure while growing up and even later in life. Therefore, I've often wondered whether her becoming pregnant was the perfect opportunity for her mother to disown and leave her to be cared for by the wider society – a society that, unfortunately, was not sympathetic to my mother's circumstances.

I have no record as to why and how my mother became pregnant. All I remember in connection with this is that I once overheard a conversation between neighbours who thought I was asleep. I was about ten or eleven years old and, at the time, living in my second children's home. I gleaned the following from that evening:

My father-to-be was a Frenchman; they even knew his name and described him as "tall, young and handsome". He was working for a year in a nearby village doing deliveries by bicycle for a bakery and a butcher.

And this is all I ever knew, which was certainly enough to arouse a young person's curiosity. Indeed, I became inquisitive and carried these overheard facts within me for years, never ceasing to wonder about it, and desiring to meet the man. No opportunity was ever given me to discover the truth of my early beginnings though. And so throughout my growing years and beyond, not knowing anything real about my father caused me to shut down and not pursue his existence. In fact, the other issue that contributed to my shutdown was the belief that my birth was purely an accident, which in turn numbed my emotions to finding out anything more about him. Quite frankly, it was easier to develop a belief system of 'not belonging' than to try to work out who my father and my mother were and why they had left me to be looked after by other people.

However, the story goes that my mother-to-be became homeless. Her version is that a sympathetic couple provided domestic employment for her in their home until another solution could be found. The interesting point worth mentioning here is that the wife of this couple became my godmother. I only saw her in my growing years, when I had to stay at her house because all the children of the home were sent away yearly for a holiday. I can also reveal here that the overheard conversation I mentioned earlier in this letter came to my ears through this godmother gossiping with a neighbour!

My godmother and her husband kept rabbits for business and so I became accustomed to seeing the killing, cooking and eating of these animals. At other times I had to accompany her into the woods to collect fallen leaves for the rabbits' bedding when cleaning out the hatches. A further experience I recall having to endure while living with the couple was that of having to eat every bit of food on my dinner plate; this proved a real problem as the food was very different from that which was given at the children's home. My godmother was a drunkard too! And to be honest, these and many other harsh experiences resulted in me taking a dislike to her when sent to her for a vacation.

Thinking again about my mother's situation, I sense that she must have gone through an unimaginably tough time, and of course I will never fully know what the constant condemnation over her life felt like. I personally feel that despite all opposition, she was proud of carrying a child that was going to be hers. And – you know? – I attribute this positive outlook as one of her best qualities in her otherwise troubled world.

I heard that different well-meaning people gave my mother advice regarding abortion, but she clearly decided to go ahead even though she was told that she would never be able to keep or look after the baby. Later, she was given advice to put me up for adoption; again, she refused to give permission for this to happen. In some ways, of course, it comforts me that she was heard and her opinion was taken into account on this matter.

The theme of adoption surfaced again in my life when I was around eight years old and still living under the care of the Salvation Army. This time the issue of being adopted was raised after an occasion when I was admitted with typhoid to a children's hospital. I remember this well because of being put in isolation, where I became friendly with a boy of the same age who also was in isolation for an infection. Unfortunately, our two rooms were separated by a glass wall; but before long, the kind ward sister pushed each bed close to the glass so that we could entertain each other, leading to us becoming good friends. The boy's parents were pleased that their son had found a friend while in hospital and began to enquire from the nurse who I was. The couple were rich, had two sons and desperately desired a daughter, and so it seemed that I became a potential solution to their wishes. Time passed and I returned to my children's home, and my friend returned to his home. I recollect distinctly the Christmas of that year because his father came to collect me to spend a few days with their family. From then on, for the rest of my childhood, this couple chose to love me and sought ways to have me adopted as their daughter. But my mother, whom I saw very rarely during my childhood, did not allow this to happen – and this shows me that she was proud and determined to keep her own child. On the other hand, I have often brooded over the question as to why she did not allow adoption and why there was no one overruling her decision – questions for which I have never found an answer.

Now, let us return to after I was born. My mother was given domestic employment in a Christian Community somewhere else in Switzerland. Again, I questioned in my mind, why did they place her so far away from where I was housed? But I have my suspicion that these 'kind' people might well have believed that not seeing the child would encourage the mother to forget the child. I don't know, except that this disadvantaged lady, my mother, seemed to know what belonged to her and had no intention of giving it away. I so respect her decision!

Astonishingly, throughout her life my mother knew no other way of employment than being in domestic service, which enabled her to live independently from her family. Her brothers, sister and parents never made any inquiries about either my mother or me. In fact, later on in my life, I was shown an official letter in which she was disinherited by my grandparents because of her "misbehaviour" and I, of course, never came to be an existing person in their lives. I only found out much later that my grandmother had lived well into my twenties. How I would have loved to meet them… but this was obviously something that was kept from me.

From my mother I learned that for many years she served two families consisting of two brothers with their respective wives who were sisters. One family owned a restaurant and the other were farmers, and both families lived under the same roof. The restaurant family employed my mother for all sorts of domestic work including washing up late into the night for the restaurant, or at other times helping the farm family with bringing in the hay and butchering and processing the animals. Basically, she was a maid for all tasks. On top of this, the restaurant family had two children – a boy and a girl – and very sadly, their daughter was born with physical and mental impairment. My mother, down the years, had been entrusted to take care of their child, which she handled extremely well. This resulted in the child and my servant mother becoming very attached to each other and it seemed that they belonged together. Thus, this employment stretched well into my mother's early seventies.

I remember in my late teens and early twenties being shown by my mother another side of the coin of her longstanding employment. She showed me her bedsit in the attic of the farmhouse. A shock shivered down my spine when I saw that small space with a bed, a wardrobe, table and a chair, and a small window which made the room rather dark. But to complain was not one of her habits; she loved it and called it her own. Bless her, she always struck me as a contented lady, rarely grumbling, and a true domestic servant, living and working only for her employer. As far as I could observe, she enjoyed working hard and did it with total reliability and honesty.

When I started my own employment I occasionally would meet up with my mother at her place of work. Her employment family were pleased to meet me, commenting verbally about my looks and height in contrast to those of my mother who was very short. These early visits used to feel hugely embarrassing since the family gave me the impression that they were staring at me and whispering to each other about the circumstances of my mother. And what's more, I struggled with my feelings that the 'special needs child' my mother was caring for seemed far more important to her than I did. But I accepted these circumstances and was glad that my mother found contentment in this relationship. There are many more events I could mention about her but will jump now to when she died at the age of eighty.

Her final years were spent in a residential care home in which she was extremely comfortable and content. When she died you were thirteen.

Do you remember us travelling to Switzerland for the occasion of the funeral? What a blessing and support you were at my side. Thank you so much for accompanying me on this memorable journey! We both knew that I had absolutely no knowledge of who your grandmother's blood family were, where they lived or whether they were alive, and if so, would they want to know about her death? But I cared, and I felt extremely keen to use this occasion to find out these things.

And so I took hold of my opportunity, launching out on something that I felt was long overdue. I made a big effort exploring through the local registry office as to who our relatives were, so that we could announce her death and at the same time introduce ourselves as the daughter and granddaughter of the deceased. I was fifty-three years of age. In a very short space of time it came to our knowledge that my late mother had two brothers with families and two sisters with families, who were all alive. I wrote to each with trepidation but at the same time very excited and proud to introduce ourselves as existing relatives. Unfortunately, the response was not great, but two of her brothers replied and one of them came to the funeral with his daughter, which was for me the highlight of the day. Now I was the one staring – at my late mother's brother, my uncle, and his daughter, my cousin!

My cousin tried to explain to me that she had been looking for me for years but without success. What a remark – what was she trying to convey? Could it have been that she was saying that it was not her fault that we were excluded from the entire family? Or did she feel guilt over the way my mother was treated, although she was not the guilty one? I don't know! I was not in the mood to respond to her words as I was simply pleased to have made contact with relatives. Sorting out the past was not one of my priorities on the day we laid my mother to rest from her earthly life. It certainly was not the place nor the time for it. And furthermore, in my mind, I was sure that what had been done in the past would not be my responsibility to sort out, nor was it under my control. But I realised that forgiveness of the past was a subject to be contemplated at some point in the future.

I was struggling as I considered my grandparents and many of my mother's siblings that had lived for many, many years after my birth. No-one had ever wished us well, let alone made an effort to see or know us, which was a very painful rejection at the core of my being. And yes, I have been puzzled all along by the attitude of these family members who so cruelly denied my mother's worth, purpose and the right to live because she was considered not worth knowing. Continuing in my reflections, I considered her family were the ones who missed out on enjoying their daughter, their sister, their aunty developing into a determined and self-supporting woman; doing good to others at every opportunity; taking her pregnancy serious by keeping the child; and facing her world with exceptional courage and therefore proving to be a remarkable woman, mother and grandmother.

How shall I end this letter? I think by commenting that I had to learn to honour and respect my mother for who she was, admiring her for choosing what she thought was right at the time, and therefore I came to believe that she truly was a humble and brave lady.

Finally, let me close with some wonderful and comforting words which increasingly became a sustaining and meaningful anchor as I had to work through and understand my confused emotions:

> Yet you [LORD] brought me out of the womb; you made me trust in you even at my mother's breast. From birth I was cast upon you; from my mother's womb you have been my God. Do not be far from me, for trouble is near and there is no-one to help.
>
> Psalm 22:9-11

> The LORD your God is with you; he is mighty to save. He will take great delight in you, he will quiet you with his love, he will rejoice over you with singing."
>
> Zephaniah 3:17

The Old and New Testaments state in different places that God is the defender and helper of the fatherless. I was fatherless and simply had to learn to believe that God was out to help in bringing me through my life's entangled circumstances. He was my support in sending the right people at the right time, teaching me bit by bit, through various means, how to overcome and develop into a healthy and wholesome person.

As I conclude, I consider it amazing and a privilege that I seemed to understand God's working in my life early in my childhood. His presence seemed to be real as far back as I can remember. And quite truly, strange as it might sound, I recollect being in the possession of a Bible, needles and wool, rather than toys!

My heart overflows with a deep cry of thankfulness.

With all my love,

Your Mum

Your Grandmother

*I have no memory of when and where this photograph was taken.
It looks like I was approximately seven to nine years old. The
photograph was given to me by one of the Salvation Army officers
at a later stage of my life and therefore it was likely taken while I
was in my first children's home. I rather like this image of my
mother and me looking very relaxed.*

Reflection

The following poem is extracted from my diary and chosen because of its heading: *Opportunity.* I believe opportunities are given to everyone, good or ill! And my mother turned her opportunities, despite her poor start in life, to their very best. Likewise, I do realise that you and I have the same opportunity to make good choices at every corner of our lives.

Opportunity

My name is Opportunity:
    I give opportunity
    To start anew,
    To choose aright,
    To trust me wholly,
    To step out in faith,
    To delight my heart.

Each new opportunity presents you:
    With an open field of inheritance,
    You can enter into your supplies,
    The fulfilling of your needs,
    Or the fulfilling of someone else's.

Do not be afraid of that which is new!
    Each new day, each new experience,
    Each new path, brings opportunity
    To prove the Lord your God in a new way,
    To know him as you did not know him before,
    To prove him, as he proves you,
    And to root you, more deeply, in the things of God.

Do not be afraid, but go forward
    And grasp happily new opportunities.
    Look up to the Lord your God.

See, my child, it is I.
Is anything too hard for me?
Can I not change situations and people?
And bring about my own plans and desires?
Can you not see how all is to a plan?

Author unknown

To every man and woman is given opportunity. Opportunity knocks on the door of his or her heart, to ask to enter in.

LETTER 3

"But as for me,
it is good to be near God.
I have made the
Sovereign Lord
my refuge;
I will tell of all
your deeds."

Psalm 73:28

My Childhood – One of Many

Discovering the unknown world...

My dearest Helen,

I am starting this letter by referring to and commenting on Psalm 73 and in particular the last verse, 28. This text was given to me on the day of my confirmation by the pastor of the local Evangelical Parish Church in 1954, and with it he wrote a letter of explanation as to why he chose the whole of Psalm 73 and why he crowned my confirmation day with the last verse of this psalm. Thus, I have kept this pastoral letter and translated it into English, as its content has accompanied me and played a significant part in my life.

The actual ceremony was one of the last events that took place while I was still at the children's home. It included the village boys and girls, plus the two of us from the children's home (see our photo at the end). There were only two of us that year, ready to leave our 'childhood nest' in exchange for the oncoming employment that was chosen by our house-parents.

I do remember the day very vividly. We were each dressed in black. My godmother attended but I have no recollection of my mother nor of any other significant person being present on the day. We all (village teenagers and the two of us) were aged between fifteen and seventeen and together were taught by the above-mentioned pastor on subjects such as Christian Religion and how we should apply Christian Ethics in the days and years to come. German hymns and Bible texts that we had to learn by heart all these years ago still regularly surface in my thoughts today. Looking back, I do find it odd that those of us from the children's home were never given the opportunity to attend the public village school. Yet here a door was opened for us to mix with teenagers of the same age from the village, for the purpose of the confirmation classes which spanned over a whole year. Sadly, this period of time made me acutely aware of being estranged from the other village children and left me feeling isolated.

Nonetheless, I find it incredible how this pastor knew what sort of seeds he had to sow into the soil of my life. The very fact that the content of his special letter was addressed to me and about me made me feel important. And I can only thank God that with his help I understood that if I wanted to value my confirmation text (verse 28) I would have to read the whole of Psalm 73, study it and allow its words to influence my life. Thinking back about things that had happened in the past, I realise just how appropriate the words of this psalm were, speaking at different times into my circumstances. And so, inevitably, I became more and more inquisitive about the God of the Bible, and when reading his word there arose in me an inner comfort and a sense of assurance that someone out there cared about me.

Yes, I slowly was learning, like the psalmist, that I too could pour out my troubled life to the same God. I was also pleased to learn how the psalmist arrived eventually at the conclusion that it was 'a good thing' to be seeing his situation from God's point of view; as a result of reviewing his past he decided that there was only one thing he was going to do:

> But as for me, my feet had almost slipped; I had nearly lost my foothold. For I envied the arrogant when I saw the prosperity of the wicked. … When I tried to understand all this, it was oppressive to me till I entered the sanctuary of God; then I understood their final destiny. … But as for me, it is good to be near God. I have made the Sovereign LORD my refuge; I will tell of all your deeds.
>
> Psalm 73:2,3,16,17,28

The psalmist seemed to be saying that one of his problems was that he contrasted himself with others who appeared better off than him, which nearly drove him to despair. But from the moment he approached God and poured out his dilemma, he understood that if he was near to God, it did not really matter what would happen; in contrast, if he was far from God, his perspective of life became confused and dissatisfied.

When I found myself being disturbed, such as being tempted in comparing myself with others, I aimed to follow the psalmist's example of using God as my counsellor, my home, my refuge; this kind of thinking provided building blocks that I adopted into my identity. With hindsight, I can confirm with reality that it was a tremendous boost to relate to the God of this psalm, even though in those early days I did not fully understand what God was all about. However, the outcome of creating this 'God-space' gave me a sense of inclusion. For example, I felt welcomed into his presence and discovered a shelter where I received strength; in this place I believed I was being listened to and my empty cup being filled with positivity.

Nonetheless, as I look back it seems that I developed a certain thought pattern that informed me that my physical home was somewhat abnormal as it entailed not having my own mother and father, a brother or sister, an aunt or uncle, but rather strangers who were my family! I also realised that the 'parents' were only figureheads guiding me through my childhood. Therefore, my childhood experience produced physical and emotional isolation that shaped my personality, and later in life created many issues as I grew.

In those childhood days I used to find shelter and comfort in my bed, the space where I created a make-believe family! The bed, for me, was the place in which I could cover up my face and cry, dream and wish, feel secure and sheltered and, in my sleep, could forget what I felt was missing. In contrast, although my bed felt like a shelter, at the same time I also experienced it as a lonely and isolated space as a mother figure was missing from my imaginary family. Coupling these experiences together with the words of the psalmist, it seemed to me no wonder that I felt drawn to this invisible God who offered me a home in his tangible presence, giving me a deep inner sense of being accepted, comforted and somehow loved.

As I mull over the history of these past years again, I am not surprised that I carried a stigma of isolation that accompanied me wherever I went. For the life of me, I just could not help but feel different from others, causing me numerous unpleasant episodes in unexpected situations. For example, I was extremely shy in relationship to others, keen to always put myself down because of being painfully aware that I had no personal story to tell and therefore felt numbness about it. This gradually gave rise to being secretive about my past. I presumed that if people knew who I was and where I came from, they would look down on me. This would further increase my sense of unworthiness.

As a result, I started hiding the 'past child' in a cupboard, believing that being out of sight would improve my self-image. At different events I experienced this inner child's voice crying out for attention leaving me feeling totally helpless and miserable. But at the same time, as I mentioned before, I learned to make use of my created 'God-space', bringing sparkle, light and encouragement into my confused and vulnerable world. Despite my seemingly negative circumstances, I developed an inner attitude of thankfulness which has never left me. I believe that God's sovereignty continued to illuminate my troubled path at the right time, at the right place, and with the right quantity of light, that produced real purpose to my life.

I believed that God recognised that I needed help in rebuilding my broken walls and that it had to be done bit by bit with his bricks and according to his plan. Of course, the building-up took time and became a battleground of falling and rising between what was, what is and what had to come. But 'old habits die hard'! For instance, words such as 'don't', 'must' and 'should' clung like glue to my personality, demanding that I should behave a certain way in order to be accepted by others.

Let me give you some examples of what it was like being part of a children's home set-up. These childhood and teenage years were difficult times as I grew up with so many other children, each with a different background, but we all shared a daily life under the one roof of being ordered around by house-parents and their helpers.

The team at the Salvation Army home consisted of women only and therefore there was no abiding father figure in the early formative years of my life. At around nine years of age I experienced one of my biggest emotional earthquakes because the 'authority' decided that I should be moved away from the Salvation Army home to another children's institution and in a totally different area of Switzerland. Why this change? What had I done wrong? This was my home, where I felt loved and was being nurtured, and where I belonged, but it all changed suddenly overnight. Why? It literally felt like my childhood roots were dug up, exposed to a horrendous storm, then transferred to an unidentified field with the hope that I would continue to flourish in what were new and strange surroundings.

The Salvation Army house-mother came with me and I still have her picture in my mind as a gentle, tall, blue-eyed and grey-haired caring mother figure. We all called her "Mother" and she was the person who taught us to sing, play the guitar and pray. She saw to it that all the children under her care, boys and girls, aged seven to fifteen, went to the local school. Later on in my life, she and one other team member of this home remained in faithful contact throughout their physical and praying lives.

Thus, on our railway journey to the new children's home, I was sitting next to my mother-substitute. I sobbed all the way. Let me remind you that at the time I had no idea who my real mother was. I arrived at my second home weak, confused and a frightened child, and understandably I did not settle well. I disliked the place and felt at times that I was unfairly treated. For me, this move was heartbreaking and had a negative influence on my later adult life.

My biological mother's first visit hit me like another bombshell. The visiting hours for relatives were set by the home-parents to be on a certain day, once a month. Eventually, it was my turn to meet my mother. I was about eleven years old. My inexperienced childish mind could not bear meeting up with a lady that was called my "mother". The thought of her coming stuck out like a sore wound, a hurting and perplexing sore for which I could find no bandage to sooth and cover. Therefore, I retreated into hiding at the time of her arrival. Everyone searched while shouting my name, but I remained quiet in the toilet until I had no further option but to come out and greet the lady.

At the children's home, bedrooms were shared by five to eight children and I really did not like it when we were moved by the people in charge to another bed in another room, whether we wanted to or not. We had one playground, one playroom, one washroom, one classroom. Everyone was bundled together, girls aged six to seventeen and a total of around thirty of us.

Our clothes were handed down within the home from child to child and each item was labelled with a number rather than our own name. My number was twenty-four, and on many occasions, I was called by that number rather than my name. Personally, I only ever wore second-hand clothes, which was not unusual, but what I didn't enjoy was when we were all together and had to strip off in order to try on the next size of garment. I never took a liking to this activity!

All age groups were taught together in one classroom which was based in the house. The teacher was our house-father and he only taught us basics. In the summer we had to work in the fields growing our own vegetables, and we walked in bare feet to the allotment; two girls pulling the front of a large wooden cart and the rest of us pushing on the sides and back. The cart contained all the tools we needed to till the ground. The house-father accompanied us on his bike! Oh, what a sight to the people we passed by! Were we a laughing stock to them – or did they feel pity for us?

Sadly, we girls experienced no contact with children outside the home except when we had to go to church and then the 'other children' sat with their parents and of course the two groups never met. I remember that when we girls had to walk up to the front benches of the church, all eyes were on us as we sat down. It repeatedly felt like we were on show!

Furthermore, my upbringing was very regimental, resembling a soldiers' camp. We were taught to line up for everything: our duties, food, clothing, personal hygiene and in the classroom environment. Our lives were organised in every detail.

I am also reminded of another occasion when we had to line up for a totally different kind of purpose. One summer's warm evening, the house-parents and their family were out in the garden enjoying themselves. We could hear their laughter and chats. How do you think we responded to this in our dormitory? Well, we had fun too and did not go to sleep as we should have done but entertained ourselves: we talked and laughed, hopped in and out of beds, thinking the people outside would not notice our mischievousness; but of course we were heard by the one person who was on duty and she reported us to the house-father. The following morning, we each had to stand at the bottom of our own bed and wait for the house-father to arrive on the scene. He then moved from child to child punishing us with beatings to some part of our bodies. I was hit in my face which threw me off balance on to my bed.

Having told you about this event, I need to add that this sort of punishment did not happen very often. But punishment did exist and I felt the impact of it in various ways; not so much by the house-parents, but from the employed carers. For example, there was a sewing lady who seemed to be always out to punish me. Also, there was a cook and one other person in charge of house chores; between them they were in charge of us throughout the day's activities. The sewing lady often slapped me in the face as a punishment. And on one occasion she disciplined me by locking me up in the dark loft, accessed through a wooden door followed by wooden stairs which led into the huge loft room. I would sit on a step crying and waiting to be let out again – as you can imagine, a scary and not easily forgotten experience.

One final example of life in the children's home was when Father Christmas arrived with his book under his arm from which he read out our bad deeds of the year. One year, I was the one chosen to be loaded into his sack, carried away to one of the toilets in the house where the door was locked from the outside. Once again, I was isolated and fearfully waiting to be set free.

So you might well understand that these sorts of experiences shaped my character and in some ways marred, influenced and dominated my outlook on life. But in spite of this theme of punishment in the home, I remember it was a place of safety and a reasonably caring environment.

I come to close this letter with the positive words the pastor spoke at my confirmation, namely, that the word of God would become a lamp to my feet and a light to my path as I faced the outside world. With an overwhelming sense of appreciation of his words, I have included his letter for you to read.

What I have written here is all in the past, and of course it is painful to recall, but my joy overrides all this with the fact that I was able to establish and create a solid family life with you and your dad. Thank you for being my daughter and thank you for continuously enhancing my life with your love,

Your loving Mum

Reflection

Surely God is good to Israel,
* to those who are pure in heart.*

But as for me, my feet had almost slipped;
* I had nearly lost my foothold.*
For I envied the arrogant
* when I saw the prosperity of the wicked.*

They have no struggles;
* their bodies are healthy and strong.*
They are free from the burdens common to man;
* they are not plagued by human ills.*
Therefore pride is their necklace;
* they clothe themselves with violence.*
From their callous hearts comes iniquity;
* the evil conceits of their minds know no limits.*
They scoff and speak with malice;
* in their arrogance they threaten oppression.*
Their mouths lay claim to heaven,
* and their tongues take possession of the earth.*
Therefore their people turn to them
* and drink up waters in abundance.*
They say, "How can God know?
* Does the Most High have knowledge?"*

This is what the wicked are like –
* always carefree, they increase in wealth.*

Surely in vain have I kept my heart pure;
* in vain have I washed my hands in innocence.*
All day long I have been plagued;
* I have been punished every morning.*
If I had said, "I will speak thus,"
* I would have betrayed your children.*

When I tried to understand all this,
    it was oppressive to me
till I entered the sanctuary of God;
    then I understood their final destiny.

Surely you place them on slippery ground;
    you cast them down to ruin.
How suddenly are they destroyed,
    completely swept away by terrors!
As a dream when one awakes,
    when you arise, Lord,
    you will despise them as fantasies.

When my heart was grieved
    and my spirit embittered,
I was senseless and ignorant;
    I was a brute beast before you.

Yet I am always with you;
    you hold me by my right hand.
You guide me with your counsel,
    and afterward you will take me into glory.
Whom have I in heaven but you?
    And earth has nothing I desire besides you.
My flesh and my heart may fail,
    but God is the strength of my heart
    and my portion for ever.

Those who are far from you will perish;
    you destroy all who are unfaithful to you.

But as for me, it is good to be near God.
    I have made the Sovereign LORD my refuge;
    I will tell of all your deeds.

Psalm 73

This is me

Mollis, in der Karwoche 1954

Das ist meine Freude, dass ich mich zu Gott halte
und meine Zuversicht setze auf den Herrn, dass ich ver-
kündige all dein Tun. (Ps 73,28)

Liebe Hanna,

kennst Du den schönen Kanon, der diesen Deinen Konfirmations-
spruch enthält? Er war im bisherigen "Mein Lied", dem Gesangbuch
der kirchlichen Jugend, enthalten. Sieh doch einmal nach. Die Melodie
passt sehr gut zum freudigen Inhalt Deines Verses.

Wenn Du Dein Leitwort recht verstehen willst, musst Du einmal
den ganzen Psalm 73 nachlesen. Dann siehst Du, dass da ein Beter
sein Herz vor Gott ausschüttet. Er sieht, wie es den Frechen und
Gewalttätigen, die nichts nach Gott fragen, gut geht. Daran kommt
er schier zu Fall. Aber je länger er vor Gott steht und frei aus
dem Herzen mit seinem himmlischen Vater redet und ihm alles sagt,
was er denkt, desto mehr wird es ihm zu einem ganz grossen Wunder,
dass er mit Gott verbunden sein darf. Mit einem Mal sieht er, wie
alles, was ohne Gott begonnen wird, elendiglich endet und sich als
Wahn und Trug herausstellt. Und dann findet er sich durch zu dem
herrlichen Bekenntnis:

Dennoch bleibe ich stets an Dir; denn Du hältst mich bei
meiner rechten Hand, du leitest mich nach Deinem Rat und
nimmst mich endlich mit Ehren an.
Wenn ich nur Dich habe, frage ich nichts nach Himmel und
Erde. Wenn mir gleich Leib und Seele verschmachtet, so
bist Du doch, Gott, allezeit meines Herzens Trost und mein
Teil.

Wie schön, wenn ein Mensch zu dieser Einsicht kommt: Wenn ich nur
Dich habe. Sieh, aus diesem Gedankengang leitet sich dann Dein
Vers her, der den Abschluss des ganzen Psalmes bildet. Es ist
dem Beter jetzt wieder die grosse Freude, dass er sich zu Gott
halten kann und seine Zuversicht ganz auf den Herrn setzt. Das
muss er allen sagen und am Ende betet er zu Gott und sagt es auch
ihm, dass die Verkündigung all seines Tuns seine Freude sei.

Jetzt verstehst Du den Zusammenhang besser. Spricht der 73. Psalm nicht auch zu Dir. Will der Herr Dich durch alles, was Dich aus frühester Kindheit begleitet- ich denke jetzt gerade daran, dass kein Vater sich zu Dir bekennt- nicht eben dahin führen, dass Du nicht mehr auf andere schaust, die leicht und glücklich fortzukommen scheinen, sondern ganz allein Deine Zuversicht auf den Herrn setzest? Ja, gewiss, will das Dein getreuer Herr. Und welch eine überströmende Freude wird Dir da zuteil. Alle Warumfragen des Psalms 73 verstummen. Nur Freude ist übrig. Wie könnte etwas anderes Dich bewegen, wenn Du an den Gekreuzigten denkst, der auch zu Dir gekommen ist und auch Dir die ganze, ungeteilte Liebe des himmlischen Vaters herabgebracht hat.

So bekenne es denn tapfer, wo immer Gott Dir die rechte Gelegenheit schenkt, dass darin Deine grösste Freude, Deine wahre, einzig dauerhafte Freude eines Lebens liegt, dass Du Dich zu Gott halten kannst und Deine Zuversicht auf ihn setzest. Gott wird Dir gewiss schenken, sein barmherziges Tun, seine Heilandstat weiterzusagen. Wie wichtig ist es doch, dass wir es denen, die Gott uns in den Weg führt und deren viele selbstsicher und protzig und deren andere verzagt und hilflos sind, verkünden, was der Herr Grosses an uns tut.

Eine Verkündigung des Tuns in Worten ist gemeint, aber auch durch die Tat. Jeder Gang zum Gottesdienst, wo dem Namen des Herrn wirklich Ehre gemacht wird, jeder Besuch einer Bibelstunde trotz dem feinen Spott der andern ist auch Verkündigung. Gott schenkt es uns auf so mannigfaltige Art, seinen Namen zu verherrlichen. Und je mehr Du dich zu ihm hältst, desto mehr siehst Du, wie Deine Zuversicht belohnt wird, wie wahr Gott ist und wie gewaltig sein ausgestreckter Arm, uns zu helfen. Und je mehr Du ein zuversichtlicher, gläubiger Mensch wirst, der sich zu seinem Herrn bekennt, desto grösser wird die Freude. Du wirst es erleben, dass sie immer grösser, immer tiefer wird. Gottes Brünnlein hat Wassers die Fülle, heisst es einmal.

Nun geh mit Deinem getreuen Herrn und sei ihm von Herzen anbefohlen. Dein Pfarrer J. Rey.

> But as for me, it is good to be near God;
> I have made the Sovereign Lord my refuge;
> I will tell of all your deeds. (Ps.73:28)

Dear Hanna,

Do you know the lovely canon that contains this Bible
text given to you on the occasion of your Confirmation? It is
included in "Mein Lied", the song-book used in our youth
fellowship. Look it up! The tune fits admirably to the cheerful
content of your Bible text.

If you want to understand your text properly, you must
first read the whole of Psalm 73. You will then see that the
psalmist is pouring out his heart to God in his prayer. He sees
the prosperity of the wicked and violent people who do not
inquire after God. This almost causes him to fall. But the
longer he stands before God and speaks freely to his heavenly
Father from the depth of his heart, telling Him
all his thoughts, the more he becomes aware of the very great
wonder that he is able to be united with God. All at once he
sees that anything which is undertaken without God ends
miserably and turns out to be delusive and deceptive. And then
he finds his way through to the wonderful confession:

> Nevertheless I am continually with You; You hold me by
> my right hand. You will guide me with your counsel, and
> afterward receive me to glory. Whom have I in heaven but
> You? And there is none upon earth that I desire besides
> You. My flesh and my heart fail; but God is the strength
> of my heart and my portion forever.

What a joy when a person comes to this conclusion: Whom
have I in heaven but you! Note well: this is the line of
thought that leads up to your verse, which marks the end of the
whole psalm. For the psalmist in his prayer it is a great joy
again to be able to draw near to God and to put his trust
entirely in the Lord. He must tell this to everyone and in the
end, he prays to God and tells Him too of the joy of
proclaiming all His works.

Now you can understand the context better. Does Psalm 73
not also speak to you? Is it not precisely the Lord's intention
through everything which accompanied you from your earliest
childhood – I am just thinking that no father declared himself
to you – that you no longer look on others who appear to be

getting on easily and happily, but that you put your entire trust in the Lord? Yes, I am sure that is what your faithful Lord intends. And what overflowing joy He thus bestows upon you! All the whys and wherefores of Psalm 73 are stilled. Nothing but joy remains. How could you be moved by anything else when you think of Christ crucified who came also to you and brought you the whole, undivided love of your heavenly Father?

And so, confess bravely, wherever God gives you the right opportunity, that this is your greatest joy, the true and only lasting joy of your life, namely that you can stand by the Lord and that you put your trust in Him. God will surely give you occasion to tell others about His merciful deed, His work of Redemption. How important it is, after all, that we declare to those whom God puts in our way – many of whom are proud and self-confident, while others have lost heart and are helpless – what great things the Lord does in our lives.

A testimony in words is meant, but also in deeds. Each time you go to church, to a service where the name of the Lord is glorified, each time you go to a Bible-study meeting despite the scorn of others, is also a testimony. God gives us so many different occasions to glorify His Name.

The more you stand by the Lord, the more you see how your trust is rewarded, how true God is and how powerful His outstretched arm is to help us. And the more you become a trusting, believing person, confessing your faith in the Lord, the greater will be your joy. You will live to see that it becomes ever greater, even deeper. The river of God is full of water, as the bible says.

So, go with your faithful Lord. I commit you to the grace of God. Your minister,

J. Frey

Translation: Hansjürg and Elisabeth Frick-Suter

LETTER 4

"…so then, just as you have received
Christ Jesus as Lord,
continue to live in him,
rooted, and built up in him,
strengthened in faith as you were taught,
and overflowing with thankfulness."

Colossians 2:6

What Will Become of Me? – Facing Reality

The past and its influences...

My daughter,

In a past notebook I found the following phrase written by Leslie D. Weatherhead (1893-1976) and its words are appealingly fitting to the subject of this letter:

Nothing can happen to you that God cannot use for good.[2]

This quotation reminds me of an experience that happened when I was fourteen and its potential could either have been damaging or affirming to my future outlook on life. Looking back, the unpleasant occurrence stung like a painful bee-sting but its discomfort did not hold me back. Instead, it had some positive effects on my unknown and frightening future. Eventually, I was drawn to Weatherhead's quote as an affirmation that God would use my negative experience for my future good, but obviously this belief did not form overnight.

So let me pause here and turn to this unique experience that took place in my second children's home, where the following conversation took place in my hearing. It was a Christmas Day when we, the children, performed to a grown-up audience, because the house-father was a local musician and loved showing off our singing and acting. We became accustomed to providing this sort of entertainment to the outside world. After the performance, as usual we withdrew to our own playroom. The room was small for the number of children it had to accommodate. I do not remember the meal we had or any kind of presents we might have received on that day. But I do remember the event that followed the presentation.

The ritual was that our guests were shown around the house and through our playroom, and some of the guests would typically chat to one or two of the girls. On this occasion the house-mother and one of

---

our guests paused exactly where I was sitting on the floor. They did not talk to or with me but conversed to one another in my hearing. The visitor posed the following questions to the house-mother:

"What becomes of these children?"

"What are the chances they have in their lives?"

"What will become of them when they leave?"

The visitor was obviously concerned about our future and had asked something that deeply resonated with me: *yes, what will become of me when I leave this place?*

The house-mother's answer shocked me in a way that made me sit up and wonder about my future. She spoke in a casual manner, so that her tone as well as her words underlined the fact that we would not be much good for anything except falling into the same trap as our parents, whose lives had been messed up in one way or another... She went on to say that we would only be capable to go into service. The house-parents would be seeking reputable families who would employ us as their servants.

I did not fully understand the meaning of it all but really felt that I had a hopeless future. Sadly, I had no-one to talk to about what I heard and therefore stored my anxious thoughts in my heart. (As a consequence of hearing this conversation, I was motivated years later to engage in writing my story with a theme like, "Can anything good come out of me?")

On the one hand, I had been made to feel no good, emphasising a low expectation of my future. On the other hand, a strong 'desire' welled up within me, like 'water to a dry garden', nourishing and lifting my spirit towards a flicker of hope; I found myself saying to someone or something outside of myself, "I will show them that I am not like 'everyone else'. I will do well with my life. I will train for a job against all odds." To me, it felt like someone had dropped a good seed with its potential into the soil of my life.

Some two years later I had a similar experience that challenged me about my future. It happened on my confirmation day. My local pastor exposed the vulnerability of my life, but at the same time encouraged me with loving and sympathetic advice to learn to trust God for what lay ahead. His prophetic words into my life were amazing! (Remember what I wrote about this in my previous letter to you.)

I came to call these glimpses of my future 'God-moments'. "Nothing can happen to me, that God cannot handle for good." Thus, I chose to believe the sound of these words. And on reflection, it is incredible that these two brief experiences provided a sense of something outside myself that pressed me to accept that God the Creator was truly on my case.

My First Employment

I was discharged from my second childhood home in my late teenage years. As part of this new imminent horizon, I was simply issued with a full set of clothes which I had partly made myself, some toiletries and a suitcase box in which to put my belongings. My future salary was to be monitored by one of the house-parents and it meant that I could not buy anything without their permission until I was eighteen.

The whole process of leaving and arriving at another place filled me with extreme nervousness. The new position chosen for me was with a family of eight people where I had to learn to serve in every household chore. Consequently, very dramatically, I became an employed citizen in a world of which I knew absolutely nothing. It truly was a frightening period and I would not wish it on anyone!

I underwent emotional stress and utter loneliness. For a considerable time, I felt very confused regarding my identity and I often cried. In those days no one wanted to know about your tears, but if someone did notice them, I was simply told, "Pull yourself together."

The wife of the family was to be my teacher in all the skills I had to acquire to become a good manager of household work as well as overseeing my attendance at college while training in Domestic Science. But very unfortunately for her and for me, she caught meningitis during her third pregnancy and became totally paralysed! Her son was born into these circumstances, and in due time baby and mother returned home, being looked after by a residential nurse. The grandmother also moved in with her dog. The rest of the household consisted of two other children aged eight and five, and a husband who was director of the bank that was situated on the first floor of the family home.

So here I was, in the midst of this large and complex household, learning fast to serve and how to become part of their lives. Believe me, I had great difficulty in knowing how to understand and process my feelings, and whenever alone, I would cry in my loft bedroom which became my refuge. The room had two round windows set in the sloping ceiling, and when standing on a chair, I could just about pop my head through to view the outside world. Emotionally and physically, although my bedroom felt like a shelter, it also felt like I had been transported from one confined place to another.

I worked every day of the week except on Sunday afternoons, and then I simply did not know how to manage my brief free time. I had no television, radio or books and therefore wondered often, how could I venture into the big wide world? And if I could, where would I go? I did not know a single person apart from the family I served; I had never gone shopping and was extremely shy. I shiver when I reflect on those distressing late teenage years. Much was expected of me and it's really difficult to find appropriate words to express the truth of it all. But – and here comes another 'but' of my life – somehow, I knew how to work hard and persevere in the midst of personal pain.

Thankfully another 'God-moment' sprinkled encouragement into my life. It was a Sunday afternoon, when I was lingering in my bedroom, brooding over what to do with my given free space. Should I or should I not go out? In the end I placed a chair in position, stood on it and put my head through the window, viewing the world I was dreading to meet. And – *wow!* – to my surprise, music reached my ears that I recognised instantly! The familiar sound drew me out of the house as fast as I could go. With my eyes and ears on high alert, I walked through the streets seeking to follow the music that led me eventually to a park where Salvation Army members were holding an open-air meeting, a sight I remembered well from my earlier childhood. Can you imagine that my whole being was drawn to this event like a bee zooming to blossom, that I found myself drinking in the consoling words and music like nectar? Yes, it refreshed and spoke tenderly into my circumstances and my thoughts wandered to the years when I had been raised under their care! It was an incredible moment; in front of me, a door of hope had opened and I sensed that I could find new feeding pasture for my life ahead.

You see, my perception of reality at that time was that seeds of discouragement seemed to take root quicker than seeds of hope. But on this day, I was given fresh encouragement to put my trust in the seed of hope. It definitely felt like a breakthrough from darkness into light. Marvellously, from that day onwards, I knew how to spend my free Sunday afternoon; namely, in the park with the Salvation Army. It became my newfound 'God-spot' where I occupied myself with listening to and observing this group of people speaking about and singing of God.

The day arrived when I followed the Army crowd to their meeting place. To do this I had to ask permission from the family as they sometimes needed me in the evening. Thankfully, they had no problem with it. The sum total of this adventure was that I became a regular attendee on Sunday evenings.

Eventually, in one of these meetings I stood up and walked forward in answer to the call from the pulpit to become a Christian. At their invitation, I knelt down at the 'sinners' bench' with a Salvation Army person beside me who encouraged and helped me to confess my sins in order to be forgiven and accept Jesus Christ into my life.

While kneeling I felt unaware of my own 'sins' but rather felt conscious of everyone else's sin being committed against me. Anyway, as I rose from the bench, I was declared by faith to be 'born again' into God's family. From this declaration, I understood and believed that Jesus had found me and his Holy Spirit had entered my empty, troubled and needy life with sparkles of assurance that he loved me and was going to work with me and I with him. From now on, I belonged to him, whom I had not seen but chose to believe, and as a result felt embraced with comforting assurances that I was no longer on my own. True enough, from that day, I sensed a deeper understanding of God's presence in my life that generated a gladness and willingness to trust him. He in turn would graciously, little by little, reveal himself to me by giving me a peace that passed all understanding and enabled me to positively grasp that God was for me rather than against me.

"Can anything good come out of my life?" Fully convinced, I could now reply with a resounding, "Yes!"

However, despite this wonderful 'God-moment', I was not automatically cured from my complex emotional life issues. Looking back, I can testify that from the day I gave my life to Jesus, my view of myself initially grew poorer before the healing of memories could progress. But as ever, I desired to get 'better and not bitter'. Hence, I have many stories of how the God-given seed, step by step, developed my potential.

This 'seed' I have written about is a really special one, as neither I nor anyone else could have bought it in a shop; rather, it was given as a gift from the maker of heaven and earth! Graciously, he was taking charge of my growth, leading me from seasons of rejection to acceptance, from hopelessness to hope, from fear to peace, from death to life, and eventually bringing me to recognise and accept the words that are recorded in Psalm 139:4: that I am truly beautifully and wonderfully made.

I will close this letter with the following amazing text that was given to me when being enrolled as a soldier of the Salvation Army:

> *But by the grace of God I am what I am, and his grace to me was not without effect. No, I worked harder than all of them – yet not I, but the grace of God that was with me.*
>
> *1 Corinthians 15:10*

What fitting and encouraging words they were for a life like mine.

They had the power to reveal a future in which God would work faithfully with and in me for his Glory. *Thank you, Lord! Amen!*

I greet you wholeheartedly,

Your Mum

March 1957

Reflection

But God…

For years, I have been observing and learning about the powerful 'buts' written in the text of the Bible. There are an amazing number of individual people and stories whose lives have been changed because of the implications of the 'buts'. Thus, I have been and always will be keenly looking out for the buts of God in the Bible, because they inspire me, and powerfully influence and change for the better how I view situations. Looking through my Bible, my underlining of the 'buts' are numerous and every time I underline, I do it with a thankful heart for the potential that the word of God offers me. Here now, I will share a few concrete biblical 'buts'; you will soon see why I am so enthusiastic about them!

It appears to me that sometimes the 'but' situation is positive, but it can also change to the negative. For example, God said to Jonah, "Go to Nineveh," but Jonah ran away the opposite direction. God had a plan for Jonah (positive) but Jonah did not like it and deliberately went the other way (negative) – *but* God persevered and finally brought Jonah to the place where he wanted him. The same scenario can take place in my life when God is encouraging me through his word to "go", to "believe", to "persevere", but just like Jonah I choose to walk in the opposite direction.[3] My belief is that God's blueprints or plans are always positive, even if in certain circumstances I don't grasp straight away the meaning of his purpose. At other times, when the 'but' seems negative it can alter things to the positive as I trust in God's authority and faithfulness.

Another example is about Joseph, one of Jacob's sons, who became a very prominent figure in the Old Testament. He served at some point in his life in the court of Potiphar, the captain of the palace guard of Egypt, and the reason why he landed in this high position was partly because his brothers were jealous and tried to get rid of him, but

---

[3] See Jonah 1:1,2

God took care of him. Among other things, we read in Joseph's story that Potiphar's wife fancied him and therefore she tempted him daily to sleep with her.

> *...but he refused her. 'How could I do such a wicked thing and sin against God?' he replied.*
>
> Genesis 39:9

In the sight of God, Joseph made the right decision, but as a consequence of not sleeping with Potiphar's wife, he was wrongly accused and thrown into prison. He lost his position and his reputation (negative) *but* again God was the strength of Joseph's heart, and while in prison God Almighty turned evil to good and raised Joseph back to an even higher position in the king's court.[4] This remarkable story teaches me to hold on to God's truth even in negative circumstances and believe that God knows the plans he has for me and that my job is to simply trust him.

I love the story of Ruth in the Bible who had the choice after her husband died to go back to her own people and her own gods. In my imagination, fragile Ruth could have wallowed in her widowhood but she chose to return to a foreign land with her mother-in-law. *But* the God of Time revealed slowly his plans and purpose to Ruth that led her through amazing circumstances to another marriage that turned out to become a surprisingly significant event in the history of the Bible.[5]

Oh, how the list of the 'buts' in the Bible have endlessly influenced and brought about life-changing experiences to me! Here are just two more:

> *But as for me, my feet had almost slipped; I had nearly lost my foothold ... Whom have I in heaven but you? And earth has nothing I desire beside you. My flesh and my heart may fail, but God is the strength of my heart and my portion forever.*
>
> Psalm 73:2,25-26

---

4   See Genesis 39:6-23
5   See Ruth 1:14-16

...for God did not give us a spirit timidity, but a spirit of power, of love and self-discipline.

2 Timothy 1:7

Therefore, in my view, it has become vital to learn to apply the power of the word of God into every situation and I have no doubt that the 'buts' will be significant for the rest of my life. I am profoundly thankful for having discovered this wonderful word and its significance in Scripture.

It is true that I am not yet where God wants me to be, but I am on his way and I am determined to listen, believe and obey his voice against all the other voices. I realise too, that God may take away, but will restore us with something better. Thank you, Lord!

LETTER 5

"I pray because I can't help myself.
I pray because I'm helpless.
I pray because the need flows out of me all the time –
waking and sleeping.
It doesn't change God – it changes me."

C. S. Lewis (1898-1963)

Nursing Training – Surprised by Joy

Reaching the unthinkable...

Dear Helen,

Singing and making things with my hands used to be two of my childhood strengths. I recollect the time when, at a very early age, we were gathered for group singing and there were occasions when I was encouraged to sing at different events. Hence, singing was very much part of my childhood. I am so grateful for the wonderful and constructive impact The Salvation Army had in my life, first when I was ten days old and then in my late teenage years (as I explained in my previous letter). I also started to be comforted in believing that God, the Creator of heaven and earth, put me together "in my mother's womb" (Psalm 139). Furthermore, I have come to believe that my coming into this world was not really an accident in God's sight, but that he was present when I was formed and born in secret.

As a consequence of this belief, I have been helped in developing an anchor-like relationship that has kept my 'life-ship' on course. I see God as the captain who is continuously navigating my 'life-ship' to his destination. And yes, one of his routes brought me back into contact with the Salvation Army when I was vulnerable, naive, confused and overwhelmed by the unknown world. I could easily have been led astray, but instead was brought to a place of belonging and learned how to live my life with meaning and purpose. Thus, I think that the following describes my experience:

> ...therefore, if anyone is in Christ, he is a new creation; the old has gone ... it is going ... because the new has come! All this is from God...
>
> 2 Corinthians 5:17

I thank the Lord God afresh for directing me to a place where I received his gift of a new inner life, and to friends that encouraged me on my way. A family from the Salvation Army congregation took me under their wings, which at the time I regarded as God appointing 'guardian angels' for me. Their son was a year older and we became friends and started to look out for each other. In a very practical and helpful way, God used this family to make a difference in my life.

Slowly, I was introduced to all sorts of Christian outreach but obviously was limited because of my work commitments. Nevertheless, from time to time I was able to engage in different activities which I had never heard of, let alone dreamed about, but they truly brought much joy to my life. For instance, I relearned to play the guitar fairly quickly, which I used to accompany our singing on Saturday nights when going from pub to pub sharing the gospel. I also took an active part in open air meetings on Sunday afternoons and later played in the Salvation Army band... Oh, to have acquired friends and learned to play musical instruments was such fun and so inspiring!

Looking back on those few years of adjusting to a life outside the children's home, I often seriously wondered, where would I have landed if I would not have followed the call to come out of my shell and look for what I now know was my 'God-moment' in the park? Having reached the end of my teenage years, I reflected on the good news of God, who had begun to fill my insecure life immensely with great surprises and joy.

My two years of household service came to an end; and on the days of my exams I received top marks in every subject, including cooking and baking, cleaning and washing, ironing, mending clothes and sewing new garments! It was now time to move on, and at an acceptable time I decided, with the help of my friends, to look for a new job. This led me to work as a cook in a day nursery, and wonderfully this job was in the same area. The new employment suited me well because I could put into practice what I had learned. I was also happy to serve in a team of three other workers while feeling at home in the environment of children which, as you can imagine, reminded me of my own childhood.

A year later I was ready to look for a new challenge and therefore was encouraged by the Salvation Army leadership to learn French. My next employment took me to become an auxiliary nurse in a French-speaking hospital in Neuchatel, in the eastern part of Switzerland. What a scary challenge! I was very keen to learn everything that was put in my way as I was working under the supervision of an Italian ward sister. However, into my seventh month of employment she went on a three-month professional break which had an extremely discouraging effect on me. Again, I felt supported by the hospital staff and the local Salvation Army. My French improved well and I loved my work and my life. The nurse-in-charge who replaced my holiday ward sister was called Sister Marie; she had trained for three years at a Christian Nursing Training Hospital in Basle, in northern Switzerland. This was her first job as a qualified general nurse.

I continued to work under her which, with hindsight, was one of the best things that could ever have happened to me. She took a real interest in who I was, where I came from, what brought me to the job and why I had not moved on to train as a nurse. It felt uncomfortable because I did not understand why she focused on these personal questions. However, she acted out of her conviction that I had all the skill and ability to move forward and make nursing my career. She explained how and where to apply to the Nursing Training School where she herself had trained. Sadly, my answer to her was expressed from my own view of myself, in that I felt I had not a leg to stand on because of the consequences of my past.

What a drama I made when I admitted with utter shame my lack of education! I crumbled in the face of what was so lovingly put before me. I was far too shy and incompetent to apply for this training. My lack of confidence seemed like a huge, unclimbable mountain because of fear that I would be rejected by the nursing school. The pain of that was too much to bear.

But Sister Marie saw past all this and fully believed in my overall character and ability. She decided to take the application process into her own hands, so she rang the training school authority and told them our story. Her confidence that I would be accepted was also partly based on the fact that this Nursing Training School had a Christian ethos and therefore might be willing to give me a chance.

I heard that the school's standard practice was for every candidate to work for three months as an auxiliary nurse at the school before the training began. I now prayed that if it was God's will for me to work there, then I would be offered a place at short notice at the next intake of students, who would start in a few weeks' time. This request seemed impossible to fulfil, but I needed to know for sure that this opportunity for me would be God's will, and this prayer was my step of faith. I first heard that the course was full except for two available places – but joy, oh joy, I was offered a place with no condition attached except to give my notice and get ready for the move. *Wow!*

So it was absolutely clear that this was God's will for me. I was an exception to the rule: I did not have to work in the hospital for three months before the training and I did not have to provide what was a necessary qualification for accepting a student nurse for full-time training. I was simply accepted on the recommendation of this qualified nurse, Marie, and I learned afterwards that all people concerned had prayed for discernment over my case.

There you have it. You can see that once again God Almighty had a plan and a purpose for my life and I was willing to give him my yes, though with mixed emotions, to be trained as a professional nurse.

Within two months, and at the age of twenty-one, I had unpacked my belongings at the Nursing Training School. I found myself thinking back to the question that had disturbed me during my childhood: "What becomes of these girls?"[6] Now I was able to provide my own answer – one very different to the negative expectations of the house-mother. I reflected that although I had decided back then, "I will make something good of my life," now that the opportunity had come, I experienced 'cold feet', nervously wondering whether I could manage the academic side of the work. Nevertheless, I found myself deeply thankful to God that this forthcoming training would not focus on my lack of education but rather reveal my potential. Full of energy and enthusiasm, I felt in a privileged position to have the opportunity to catch up on what I had missed.

With this sentiment I started the training to become a qualified nurse. What an honour and what a challenge! At that time someone encouraged me by giving me the following words: "God gifted you with a sound mind." So I allowed my confidence to rest in his gift rather than reflect on my shortcomings. Increasingly I felt the reality that

---

[6] See Letter 4

nothing had happened to me that God could not use for his good.[7]
Praise his name!

I enjoyed living in one of the nurses' student homes that was situated in the beautiful hospital grounds. It had several bedrooms, each of which contained several beds. In my first term I shared a bedroom with seven other beginners of our forthcoming training, but despite these good surroundings, I entered a place where my emotional life was sorely tested. The reason for this was that my room-mates talked about where they came from, their family lives and schools, and naturally I found it so hard to take part in these conversations. I had no equivalent stories I could share, and that left me feeling isolated and outside the group. Feeling ashamed of my background, I decided to give away as little as possible of my story. I even started fabricating tales that made my life story sound rosier than what the feelings inside me betrayed. Eventually, I started to avoid this bedroom chatter altogether and instead withdrew into the 'prayer cabins' which were placed on the third floor of the building. This looked like a good and safe place for me, and in this secret place I learned to get on my knees and to pour my heart out to God about things I could not express to others. In addition, reading the Bible proved to be a great consolation in those days. Looking back, it seems strange how I responded to those situations. At the time it seemed to work, though, in that it helped me to keep my 'shameful' past to myself while firmly believing that God understood.

The three years of training were tough. I had to overcome many stumbling blocks, but throughout my training my faithful heavenly Father appointed some amazing individuals who privately taught me various topics that I needed to understand in order to pass my professional nursing exams. Thankfully, I had been blessed with a very practical, willing and quick-to-learn personality. These positive experiences together acted like streams of water flowing through my hidden desert land, and refreshed, encouraged and inspired me to do my utmost to obtain the qualification.

It was sad that one student nurse had to leave halfway through the training because of her unsuitability, and another one failed the exams

---

[7] Ibid.

at the end of the three years – but it was not me! The fact that I was able to make such progress was, in those days, an astonishing achievement for a young person of my background.

As I am recording these events, I can do nothing but thank God for his abundant patience in bringing me through incredible places of learning and helping me to succeed. However, the cost of success was that I lost weight. I became frail and extremely tired, so the School of Nursing provided me a holiday. Then, after enjoying the refreshing break, I returned to the hospital as a newly qualified staff nurse working under a godly sister-in-charge who often took me by my hand saying at the beginning of a working day, "Let's pray together for patients under our care."

I enjoyed being a nurse enormously and I gave it my everything. Nothing was too much! It felt very rewarding attending the sick and making them feel better. Part of the reward was that the patients simply accepted my love and my concern for them. But this particular story of my life is not complete without telling you about our forthcoming event of celebrating the achievement of our Nursing Diploma.

Parents and other relatives were invited to watch our entertainment, which was a play called *Travel to the Moon*, followed by a meal and speeches from the hospital management. I was greatly troubled when I began to think, "Whom can I invite to this occasion?" Once again, to my dismay, I managed to see only my lack of family connections, which created an inner pain and shame that I did not want others on the team to see. I had presumed that my troubled past no longer had power over me as I had become 'someone in my own right'; after all, I had qualified as a registered trained nurse and become a professional personality and, yes, I had proved that the unthinkable was achievable. Praise God! But once again I found myself feeling different from others, isolated and powerless, and all because I had no home to call my own or family members to invite (and I hardly knew my mother). The miserable, empty feelings seemed to cloud the potential excitement and joy of the wonderful forthcoming celebration.

In tears, and overwhelmed, I finally staggered to my colleagues and asked the question, "Who on earth do I invite?" We discussed it together and came to the conclusion that I could invite a Salvation Army Officer who had been faithful to me ever since my birth. Would she come? I had not seen her for some time and she lived far from where the event would take place. But we made contact, and to my delight she accepted and appeared on the day. Still, I had a niggling feeling that it might reveal to everyone present that I was a Salvation Army child, meaning that I was born illegitimate – which I continually tried to hide from others. In the end, however, the evening went extremely well and served as another step in the healing of my emotions.

After graduation, I stayed working at the hospital as a staff nurse for one year, earning a regular income. During this year one of my wishes was fulfilled. I had long carried a deep desire to own and learn to play a musical instrument, so from the money I earned I bought a flute. I chose this instrument because I could take it wherever I went. A delightful female music teacher from the local music school came with me to the shop and helped with the choosing of the instrument, and she started to give me lessons. My learning to play continued for many, many years.

I come to the end of this letter and will close with my version of a chorus that sums up my personal view of God, revealed in the person of Jesus Christ who so graciously brought real significance to my life:

How good is the God I adore,
My faithful unchangeable friend!
His love is as great as his power,
And knows neither measure nor end!
It is Jesus the first and the last,
Whose Spirit shall guide me safe home,
I will praise him for all that is past,
And trust him for all that's to come.

I greet you affectionately
and prayerfully,

Your Mum

This is me

Reflection

From my diary:

It is one thing to trust the invisible God when all goes well, but it becomes another issue when walking in a tunnel with no other view than darkness. God wants to bring out his best but I need to totally trust him with everything that is going on in my life. and it is my experience that he never disappoints. Thank you, Lord God!

I have come to the conclusion that obedience to the word of God is imperative if I'd like to see changes for the good in my life and therefore, it is equally essential to spend time and listen to what God's Spirit is saying; whether it is through prayer, reading and studying his word or through reading books, or through other people's experiences, and so on ... with God's help and my cooperation, impossible situations become possible...

Here is an example of trust and obedience that may test us to our very limits. I found in a man called Eugene L. Clark (1924-2012) who wrote a song called *Nothing is Impossible*. He too experienced a new way of expressing himself in his weakness, as his life story tells us that his fingers once flew across the piano keyboard but he later became a victim of crippling arthritis and also totally blind. This is why he entitled his song as...

Nothing is Impossible (1964)

I read in the Bible the promise of God,
That nothing for him is too hard;
Impossible things he has promised to do,
If we faithfully trust in his word.

The word of the Lord is an anchor secure,
When winds of uncertainty blow:

Though man in his weakness may falter and fail,
His word will not fail us we know.
All things are impossible, this is his word,
Receive it, 'tis written for you,
Believe in his promises, God cannot fail,
For what he has said he will do.

Creator of all things, with infinite pow'r.
He spoke! They appeared by his mouth;
Impossible things are known unto him,
He made us, he ruleth the earth.

Nothing is impossible when you put your trust in God;
Nothing is impossible when you're trusting in his word.
Hearken to the voice of God to thee:
"Is there anything too hard for me?"
Then put your trust in God alone
and rest upon his word –
For ev'rything, O ev'rything is possible,
Yes, ev'rything is possible with God![8]

Wonderful truth!

---

[8] Written by E. L. Clark

LETTER 6

"Any healing of the past has to be
brought into the present or it is a waste of time.
Just as Peter got out of the boat and took his first step
on the water, so we have to risk getting out of the
past and walking in new ways ...
We prefer to have a magic wand wafted over us
and have all our problems disappear in an instant.
Unfortunately, this would cause us
to remain immature children for ever.
The hard work involved in solving our problems
matures us and strengthens us.
We emerge from the experience
with a new self-awareness and self-respect."

With permission taken from *Set My People Free* (1987)
by Mary Pytches

Hang-ups – and Hopefulness

Avoid or embrace...

Dear daughter,

I opened this letter with a short extract from Mary Pytches' book *Set My People Free* because the lifeblood of her writing was about helping people to be set free from the past and to be walking in new ways. Reading the book helped me with what I used to call "the long, hard walk to the healing of the past". In this letter, then, I will tell you about various times and places where such healing took place in my life.

I am convinced that one such place of healing was that of my three years' nursing training. This period unquestionably contributed towards a healthier self-image. It was such a wonderful experience that I, who had once been considered a 'nobody', was given the opportunity to develop into a professional, gifted 'somebody'. Moreover, during this time I received all kinds of insights that brought healing to my mind and soul. I praise God for using different means along the road to promote his own life and work in me!

However, God's work in my life did not come to a halt once I had a profession and a place in society. In fact, at work I faced some rather uncomfortable situations in which things said or done by others in my presence hurt me deeply. Often, I did not know how to deal with what came my way and what was going on inside me. As a consequence, I tried to control my emotions mainly by blaming myself; for example, telling myself that I was too sensitive and just needed to present a strong public image and carry on with my work. But of course, in the long run this was not sufficient as it often left me feeling at a loss and isolated. Hence, my answer was to work harder and seek to please others, as I believed my acceptance depended on my performance.

At this time I thought of God, too, as hard and demanding, continuously watching and reprimanding me. How I had to learn that this was not the true nature of God! The 'must', 'ought' and 'should' that had been very much a part of my growing up years still influenced, and even sometimes dictated, my actions at my most vulnerable times. To feel accepted was overwhelmingly important to me.

Another example that threw me out of kilter at times was when I failed in areas where I thought I had learned, and my feeling of disappointment showed me that there was still much to learn about the benefit of failure. At other times, I would find myself filled with a deep, disturbing sadness, without understanding why I was feeling that way.

All these emotional issues seemed to prevent me from having a positive outlook on life. They rather tired me and gave me unwanted feelings of guilt and failure. *But* all was not lost, and retrospectively I am a positive witness to how these unwanted stumbling blocks that were set to destroy me, actively became 'God-moments' as I searched for his help. Little by little, at the right times and places, he changed my thinking, bringing practical revelation that helped me.

I learned to be a 'God-pleaser' and not to be ashamed when things went 'pear-shaped' but to hear and accept the unwanted as an integral part of my faith journey. God could turn the bad things around for good. I came to the conclusion that my background did not need to be my label but I could allow God's redeeming work in my life to be my label instead.

A certain quote sums this up beautifully:

It's the value God places upon you that's important, not what your parents think about you or anyone else.

This truth causes thanksgiving to God to well up inside me, for his just, loving and purposeful view on my life (and indeed, on all his creation).

I now move on to what happened after I completed my one-year staff nursing job at Basle. My friendship with the son from the Salvation Army family[9] had continued throughout these past years but we rarely saw each other as neither had spare money for travel. The truth at the time was that I was still on the waiting list as a candidate for full-time service as a Salvation Army Officer. The Head of

---

[9] Letter 5

Headquarters therefore gave me advice that I should discontinue this friendship since he did not have the same call to full-time ministry. I took the recommended suggestion to move and seek employment in England for one year, and after was to return to the Salvation Army college and take up the position in their training school.

Thinking back over those days, I realise that the Salvation Army had great influence on my life. The reasons were most likely that I felt at home with them; they meant a lot to me. I experienced only positive relationships and very much felt that they took the place of parents in my life. What is more, I was so convinced of my calling to become part of the Army team that I was prepared to give up everything, even my potential boyfriend. Both these relationships made me feel that I belonged and therefore to have to let go of one of them was not an easy decision to take and it was sad when my friend met me at the Basle railway station to say goodbye.

My journey took me through the night to Folkestone then across the Channel and finally to a small cottage hospital in the county of Kent. I loved living in England for all sorts of reasons. I was a twenty-three-year-old with a blossoming personality, and outwardly talking about my background became less of an issue for me.

The staff and matron at the cottage hospital were all Christians. The hospital had two floors: the young disabled female patients were on the bottom floor and the terminally ill female residents on the top floor, and these patients all needed long-term care. The whole place felt like a family set-up. The matron was a very genuine, loving and interesting person. She was concerned for all and her professional leadership was underpinned with Bible teaching, prayer and support of relatives, patients and staff. Every morning, the word of God and prayers circulated through a microphone to every room of the house. With a genuine hush the work stopped, and all seemed happy to listen and be encouraged by it. The majority of the nurses and the auxiliaries came from various European countries and a couple from Brazil. I loved it!

We, the overseas employees, were given a house to share. Each of us had our own bedroom while a very loving housekeeper came in daily to prepare breakfast and to cook a meal for those who had a day off. She did the washing and kept the house clean and garden tidy for us to enjoy. I was taken aback by the sheer practical love expressed towards us outsiders from the English – very remarkable! Who could have asked for anything more? Even the learning of the English language was integrated into our work, and surprisingly, one of the ward sisters was the daughter of Salvation Army parents who had retired as missionaries from China. I was so incredibly fascinated that wherever I seemed to move the Salvation Army was there before me; I could not escape from them even if I wanted to!

With time, this ward sister invited me to her home and I became a friend of the family spending many happy hours playing my flute with her father who played the piano, and of course I attended their church service and joined the choir whenever I had the opportunity. A lovely extra touch from being in this environment was how it helped to improve my English.

Within a number of months of employment, my certificate of State Registered Nurse (SRN) arrived and that meant that I could work and be paid as a staff nurse. Wonderful! Shortly after that I received another letter addressed to me. This time it arrived from the Salvation Army in Switzerland and contained the following question: "What is your choice, nursing or the Salvation Army?" With no hesitation whatsoever, I cancelled my plans of fulltime service with the Salvation Army, as now I had a deep inner conviction that the training to be a Salvationist in the Army was not my future. As you know, I never returned to Switzerland, but the interesting thing about this story was that my male friend whom I had had to leave behind in Switzerland actually entered full-time service with the Salvation Army while I was in my first year in England. Forty years later I met this friend unexpectedly at a reunion in Switzerland and for both of us it was an incredible 'silent moment' while reminiscing.

I am reminded of the following Bible text that certainly rings true:

Many are the plans in a man's heart, but it is the LORD's purpose that prevails.

Proverbs 19:21

The next opportunity in my career was being trained as a midwife. I applied to a hospital in Croydon and I completed the first six months successfully. I then went on to the Epsom District Hospital for the next six months. Three months of this time was spent in the hospital and three months out in the community where I was living with two well-established practising midwives. Through them, I was taught and supervised in doing home deliveries, which I found to be an exciting and fulfilling experience. I enjoyed my journeys through beautiful countryside cycling to where I had to deliver the baby. In due time, I completed the training year, passing the national midwifery exams, and I qualified as a State Registered Midwife (SRM). Thus, my overall nursing qualification became equal to the English professional standards, namely, SRN (State Registered Nurse) and SRM, and so my professional confidence increased.

Happily, I continued working as a midwife in a maternity hospital in Beckenham. But after a season I discovered that being a practising midwife involved enormous responsibilities and huge emotional strain. Therefore, I returned to my general nursing career and accepted a ward sister's post in Ealing.

The question yet again, "Can anything good come out of me?" made me remember all my helpless and hopeless beginnings, with a renewed heartfelt joy and thanksgiving for all I had been able to learn and put into practice. Slowly – and yes, so slowly – I learned to answer this question with a yes, but only because of the sustaining relationship I had with God who continuously and through various means drew me to trust his word whatever the situation.

The LORD is my light and my salvation –
  whom shall I fear?
The LORD is the stronghold of my life –
  of whom shall I be afraid?

Psalm 27:1 (emphasis added)

Do not conform to the pattern of this world [do not listen to the lies of your past], but be transformed by the renewing of your mind. Then you will be able to test and approve what God's will is – his good, pleasing and perfect will.

Romans 12:2

The meaning of these words to me established themselves as a ship's anchor, in that I continuously aimed to bring my complex thought world in line with God's will. In other words, God's view had become fundamental to my emotional and physical well-being. Hence, learning scripture by heart helped me to be focused on the truth. Thanks be to God!

Although my nursing career went well and I felt increasingly at home with patients and colleagues, I came across the possibility of becoming a student at a missionary Bible training college in Ealing. Why this possibility appeared and how I had the nerve to apply, I don't remember! But maybe it was a desire that stirred within me for a break from my professional life. Obviously, this missionary Bible training cost money, of which I had little, and becoming a full-time student again would mean that I would have even less. But I was totally up for such a challenge and applied.

The interview with the principle of the college went well. I answered plainly all the questions, and a temporary door of entry was opened, even though I had no intention of going abroad as a missionary (which was one of the criteria of being accepted) and I did not have money to pay the fees. The principle suggested that I applied for a grant to the local authority which, if approved, would be the final evidence that it was within God's plan for me to become a Bible student.

The college was called the *Missionary Training College for Women* and, amazingly, I was awarded the necessary money for the two years' residential study and training. It was an unbelievable, awesome and extraordinary opportunity.

At the time I didn't fully understand the purpose behind God opening this two-year door for me, but his purpose became clear on reflection. The very ethos of the life of the college was that everything had to be shared, which was in contrast to my experience at the nursing training school. Sharing bedrooms, mealtimes, lessons, free time, prayer and so on, became a point of stress for me – meaning that I needed to find a way to cope, and God had the opportunity to work on a new area of my life.

At first, I started to pretend, or cover up these feelings, as best as I knew how, because the proper way to face my problem did not occur to me at the time. My issue was that wherever I went, there were always people who were talking, sharing, being community, but I, on the other hand, found myself awkwardly standing alone in the midst of everyone else. Even my well-acquired professional attitude went out of the window. Small things became blown out of proportion; like meal times where I struggled to eat because I simply felt sick, sitting with so many people at one table. Each table had about eight to ten students and a lecturer at the end. Lots of talking was going on about all sorts of subjects and, for the life of me, I could not figure out where I fitted in or how to engage in the conversations. Hence, I sat at mealtimes like a squashed melon.

Why was I not in control? Why did I feel isolated, different from others, troubled and wounded, in a place where a godly atmosphere reigned? What was it that disturbed and spoiled circumstances?

Thank God, after a period of time, one of the live-in tutors noticed my behaviour. In fact, all the staff became concerned and so I was invited one day to her room. From that day on, we met on a regular basis. I was deeply touched that there was someone who thought it helpful for me to verbalise layer by layer the hurts of every kind that had settled in my thought-world. She had the ability to question deep into my heart and I responded freely, hiding nothing. In fact, the whole counselling experience was immensely consoling rather than making me feel guilty and ashamed as had been my past experience.

I recall, for instance, a question that bowled me over at the time. Regarding the children's home, she asked, "How many children slept in the same bedroom?" Why she was interested in such details was totally beyond me, but it felt very reassuring. Consequently, my childhood memories poured out of my mouth unhindered and – oh, joy – it was truly healing to sit and talk in her presence. Her loving probing into my history felt like she had accepted me and my past without judgment, resulting in a reassured self-image.

However, at that time my physical body responded with a duodenal ulcer that caused pain and temporary mental depression. I also regretted being unable to attend lectures and had to rest from community life until I was stronger.

Looking back now, I can understand that the college was a God-appointed place to learn more of what was meant by being changed from the inside out. I believe that he taught me:

- that he does not bring liberty all at once but in his wisdom deals with one area at a time so that his work can be done thoroughly and so that we learn to lean on him;
- that he uses other people, their prayers and his word to bring a growing maturity into our Christian walk;
- that we must learn to be able to accept love from others. When I did this, it increased my understanding of the love of God for me: he loved me first and he willed that I should live a purposeful life here on earth.

I came to believe that all these different experiences at the college were a gift from God. He initiated the healing, but I had to do the trusting and obeying.

From what I experienced during this and other times, I know that I need to always press on, living the truth and co-operating with God's word. I realise, too, that he has not finished with me yet, but it's reassuring to sense that I am walking in the right direction – *his* direction. I believe with all my heart, mind and soul that God is faithful and has started a good work in me which he will bring to completion.

After my two years at Bible college I felt drawn back to work at the same hospital and, true enough, they re-employed me as a staff nurse followed by promoting me to be a ward sister. The college staff remained a home-like anchor who prayed and provided a listening ear when I needed one. As you know, later I met your future dad in this hospital. The college staff remained faithful and, like a family, supported me and attended our wedding.

Finally, I close this letter with a prayer of acknowledgement found in a past diary:

Jesus, you are changing me. By your Spirit you're making me like you. Jesus, you're transforming me, that your loveliness may be seen in all I do. You are the potter and I am the clay, help me to be willing to let you have your way. Jesus, you are changing me, as I let you reign supreme within my heart.[10]

---

[10] written by Marilyn Baker, who gave me permission to reproduce this here

With love,

Your Mum

Reflection

The following is another piece of my creative writing which endeavours to express thoughts and experiences on paper:

Chosen for Good

God's Spirit said:
"But you, my child, my friend and my sister,
Remember
how I chose Jacob long ago;
how I placed Abraham in a land he did not know;
how Samuel heard and followed my call
and Mary's willingness to give birth to the Son of God.
Believe me, my child,
you too are chosen for my purpose alone."

And I replied:
"I choose to believe
that you saw my unformed body,
you were awake when I was made,
and wove me gently together,
raised and gave me my name.
You hand-picked me, made me unique and precious,
inscribed me into the palm of your own hand;
later, led me through turbulent waters
and lifted me out of the sinking sand
as your own loved child!
How I love and accept your creativity.
Precious are your thoughts to me,
more than gold or silver in my hands.
Mysterious, yet your loving gift is real;
you changed my clothes from Old to New;
thank you for creating me anew;
I pray, help me to live within your will."

During my nursing training,
we often engaged in singing and playing the guitar

LETTER 7

"Progress means getting nearer to the place
you want to be. And if you
have taken a wrong turning, then to go
forward does not get you any nearer.
If you are on the wrong road, progress means
doing an about-turn and
walking back to the right road; and in that
case the man who turns back
soonest is the most progressive man."

Mere Christianity (1952)
by C. S. Lewis (1898-1963)

Recovering Lost Ground –
Discovering Family Life

Old belief systems die hard...

Helen, my daughter,

I love the subject of history and the fact that I too now have a family history that I can associate with. By this I don't mean just because I met my blood relatives on the day of my mother's burial.[11] Rather, I mean that I found myself as part of a real and meaningful family with your dad and you. So with a joyful heart, in this letter I will look back at your birth and some of the events of your childhood that influenced our lives as we received you into our midst. What a gift you were and are! And what a pleasure it is to record a part of your story and pass it on to you!

As you arrived on the scene, your dad and I had to learn to adapt as your life was added into our physical and emotional living space. It meant that I needed to learn to juggle time and energy between you, your father and my social life. Cultural differences from having grown up in a different country surfaced, and sometimes revealed new things that I needed to learn in order to enhance our family life. Each responsibility brought different demands and expectations, which at times created conflict in our marriage that we endeavoured to work out. When I wronged him, I needed to return to acknowledge and apologise – and learn to implement the right approach in order to be at peace.

Some of these lessons were more enjoyable than others. Let me give you an example that might come as a surprise to you, but for me at the time was extremely important. The fact was that I had no recollection of nursery rhymes nor knowledge of children's stories, and this created in me a feeling of inadequacy as a mother. As a result, it became of utmost importance to me to learn the various words and

---

[11] Letter 2

melodies so that I could sing and read them to you in a meaningful way. I enjoyed every bit of that kind of motherhood-learning.

My personal allocation of time was another issue. I needed wisdom so that no-one would be left out from our extended family or wider circle of friends. At the time, we lived around the corner from the local hospital where I had worked (and met your dad). I had started a Hospital Nurses Christian Fellowship (HNCF) when I worked there, and continued to attend after I got married. Therefore, a number of student nurses came to visit us regularly. Then you came along and I could no longer attend the fellowship at the hospital, but my lively friendship with the nurses continued. At their request, I hosted regular Bible study evenings in our home and our front door was open during the day to any of them. The attraction for them to come to a family environment was great, and to be able to cuddle our baby was a bonus. I have wonderful memories of time well spent with these friends. They brought added joy into our household and my input continued during the first year of your life. (After that, the leadership of the group was taken on by another nurse, so the fellowship was moved back into the hospital.)

Before I continue writing about your first year of life, let me briefly pause and look back to the developing and nourishing friendships I had with the student nurses while I worked as a ward sister in their midst. We had endless meals together as most of the nurses were of Chinese origin and they simply loved communal eating. After the meal followed Bible studies to which every nurse in the hospital was invited. Their devotion to their Christian faith was commendable. They never stopped talking of what Jesus meant to them, and as a result many student nurses came to trust in the message of the gospel of Jesus Christ. We also had holidays together for the purpose of studying the Bible, fellowshipping in prayer and enjoying social activities. On one occasion, we joined the Chinese church in London for a Bible teaching conference held in Ashburnham Place, Sussex. This was a truly wonderful and meaningful time and packed with love and care for one another and the people around us. Some years later, several of these students returned as qualified nurses to their homeland; some married and continued in their profession. However, as a consequence of our friendship, you might remember that you and I received an invitation to visit them and their families in Malaysia. (I think you were around seventeen years old at the time.) They gifted us with a ticket to fly to Kuala Lumpur where we stayed for a few days with three different families. Furthermore, they organised and paid for a few days' stay in Ipoh, Perak, and a few further days on the Penang Island of the Malay Peninsula. For both of us, this holiday was an amazing and unforgettable adventure in which we were showered with generosity, love and respect, making it quite clear (and to my delight) that I had become their sister, not only at work but also in Christ. *Thank you, Lord God!*

But let's now continue to remember the highlights of your first year of life and beyond.

There was Aunt Rösli from Switzerland who came and gave me support in looking after you and our household. As you know, she was one of the mother figures who had looked after me[12] when I was a baby and I had grown up under her guardianship until the age of nine years. Her love, care and prayer for me continued all the way until she died. Hence, her visit at this time was a very special occasion, a privilege that she would now see my baby, holding and loving you with the same love that she had offered me all those years previously. Later in your childhood, she was the person who regularly posted us Christmas parcels. Do you remember how she used to wrap up every individual gift? Most of them were hand-made by her and useful, thus making our unpacking an exciting venture. Oh, she was such a lovely and thoughtful Salvation Army person!

The year 1975 came to a close; you were three months old and, as was a habit of mine, I reflected back on the year, remembering particularly that I had survived two operations during the pregnancy. (As a result, I have never stopped marvelling that you were born alive and well, in what were for us 'fragile circumstances'[13].) To celebrate the end of the year we had an invite from your dad's oldest sister and her husband to join us with their daughter and husband. As we entered the house, your dad carried you in your carry-cot, fast asleep, and he placed

---

[12] Letter 3
[13] Letter 1

you on the settee. Your dad's brother-in-law (your Uncle Stan) came and admired you. But very sadly, our evening did not turn out as we expected. Apparently, your uncle Stan had not been feeling well all day and a short time after our arrival he had a heart attack and died before the ambulance arrived. It was such a tragic event that it was hard to believe it was all real. His wife had already lost her first husband during the war and his daughter, your cousin, lost her father very suddenly and unexpectantly on this sad evening. Stan was a genuinely lovely man who always very affectionately made me feel welcome at every family gathering. Your dad treasured his friendship; they got on really well together and therefore this loss left a big hole in your dad's life.

So 1976 had a disturbing beginning – but life had to go on. And as a couple, we continued to be totally absorbed in your development. You were an amazing distributer of joy to everyone who met you and so perfectly created, nothing was missing; your smile was gorgeous; you cried easily like any other child would; you continued well with eating and drinking; and you settled in your bed contentedly. Your dad, in those days, had a special name for you: "Chuckle", meaning 'smiler'.

Moving on with our lives, we declared our thankfulness for the gift of your life by dedicating you to the Giver of Life. This dedication was done at our local Baptist church where we had got married. There, in front of a crowd of friends and relatives, we promised to bring you up in the Christian faith to the best of our ability. Your dad and I made this decision to dedicate you, rather than have you baptised, so that later you could make your own choice whether to follow Jesus. The whole celebration was crowned with joy and thankfulness to God with family and friends.

Another highlight of your first year worth mentioning was the time spent on holiday in a hired boat on the River Thames, which was in so many different ways a marvellous family experience. For example, your dad absolutely loved being at the steering wheel; ducks rested repeatedly on the windowsill of the boat as if to say that they wanted to share our journey. Bathing you in the tiny 'boat kitchen sink' was a cute experience; you also slept very well in the carrycot, which was a great relief to us. As you will well remember, we regularly had this kind of holiday during your childhood, through which you were just as delightful.

Another event to remember was the arrival of your Swiss grandmother. This reminded me of our wedding day, which had been her first visit to England; at that time she had stayed with good friends of ours, and I had seen very little of her because these friends took care of her from arrival to departure. Now, somewhat anxiously, I realised that this time she would be staying under our roof, which meant that we would be together for the first time in our entire life. I wondered how it would work out. However, I did not need to worry one iota. Your dad was amazing with his mother-in-law even though she did not understand a word of English; he knew exactly how to show respect and put her at ease. They played endless card games together, and other times she occupied herself for hours with building houses out of Lego which she bought for you. (In fact, your dad and I suspected that she might well have purchased the toy because *she* wanted to play with it! Whatever the reason, it was a delight to watch her being happy and content, and it also meant that she felt at home.) Your grandmother also enjoyed buying dolls. Do you remember the doll with blue hair called "bluey"? You carried this doll around with you for years. So all these different expressions of her seeming content spoke to me of a lovely lady who had learned to be humble, thankful and unassuming. Her visit truly served as a bonding phase for me as I finally found the opportunity to acknowledge her with love and was proud of the way she lived out her motherhood. I did have a few more chances to meet up with her when we visited Switzerland, but these occasions were always short since she was unable to provide hospitality for a longer stay.

In December 1978, you were three years old and with that another significant landmark shaped our future lives as we moved out of London to a new home in Berkshire. What a month to move! The weather was cold and miserable; we knew no one but eventually connected with a local church and subsequently were visited by its pastor, who helped us settle in the area.

The following springtime you fell ill unexpectedly with tonsillitis followed by swollen ankles and coloured patches on your skin, and to make things more difficult, we were away in Sussex but decided on that morning to cut short the visit and travel as fast as we could back home. I was particularly worried because of the swollen ankles and the blue skin rash... I sensed that it had something to do with your blood and was very concerned. When we got home, I immediately phoned the doctor, who responded by coming and examining you, but was unable to identify the illness. The ambulance was called, and you and your ill and painful body were driven to the local hospital where different tests were carried out, lasting through to the next day. Finally, the paediatrician came to the conclusion that you suffered from *Henoch-Schönlein purpura* (HSP) – a rare condition in which blood cells and vessels become inflamed, and which typically results in a rash, swollen joints and stomach pain, and could affect people of any age although the majority of cases occurred in children under ten. We also learned that HPS was caused by a problem with the immune system, possibly as a result of your tonsillitis. I stayed at the hospital with you, and after a few days we returned home with a follow-up appointment for a blood test. In time, however, your health picked up and all was declared normal. How thankful we were!

Your primary school followed at the age of four and the school building was only a few yards from our house, giving you the opportunity to come home for lunch, which we both enjoyed.

Now, let's move fast forward to when our home situation started to change again, when you were approximately eight-and-a-half years old. This time it was because of your dad's early retirement from his much-loved railway company. A good year into his retirement, an opportunity arose for a gardener's job at a private Christian conference centre outside Henley. It looked glamorous, exciting and offered a promising future, which we as a couple embraced with great anticipation as it would bring work for your dad and offer a new start for us as a couple.

But what did it mean for you? You sadly had to leave behind your school friends, your home and our much-loved dog, for which we had to find new owners. You shed many tears over the loss of our dog. I have no doubt whatsoever that the actual upheaval and changes were a disturbing experience for you. But once we arrived and you settled into the new environment, you shouldered 'the new' very well and discovered opportunities to build friendships which lasted well into your teenage years and beyond.

The owners of the Christian conference centre community lived in a great country house standing in a huge garden. 'The Lodge', situated close to the woods, became our new home, and there was another family with two children living in a pretty cottage on the other end of the estate. Somewhere else in the grounds stood a rundown building that was used as a games room, and during our community-serving time it was demolished and replaced with a small but magnificent theatre-like building for the purpose of reaching out with a range of well-planned activities to a wider community. At the time of our joining the community it consisted of a fulltime housekeeper, the family from the cottage, the family who owned the estate, and us. For a number of years, the owners made their home available for hospitality to church groups, individual Christian leaders and varied conferences. Clearly their work was cut out, and plans for future expansions of programmes were imminent. Almost overnight your dad became the gardener and handyman. I, with time, was invited to help wherever there was a need: kitchen, cleaning, gardening, local Bible study and various other functions linked to the local church – and not to forget that I also had responsibilities as a mother and a wife. I was quite eager to be part of this new expression of living together and enjoyed the challenges that came my way. In no time at all, I had developed into a successful multitasker!

One of the big projects we became part of was that under the owner's guidance and that of other experts, the eight acres were developed into a wonderful, horticulturally interesting and spacious garden. When this project came to completion it influenced further expansion of our programmes, for example, organising and leading 'Quiet Days' to which the Christian public flocked like ducks to water. But of course, this all meant careful planning and delivery, and so one programme followed another.

Life became extremely busy and my involvement was more than I had bargained for. Months and years came and went during which I was given many opportunities to assist with various projects, household chores and gardening. Together these stretched my mind and tested my physical and emotional abilities. The daily workload frequently spilled over into evenings and weekends, giving me the experience that much was expected, and sadly, I feel the Christian community work took priority above all else. I grew tired and at times worked against my will.

My emotions suffered and I felt confused as to who I was and where my priorities lay. This resulted in silent stress and a growing negative feeling that I was not coping very well – but the work had to go on. My well-meaning community spirit became progressively strained, resulting in working even harder in order to satisfy my rising need to please others, rather than speak up and face the truth of the situation. There was no doubt that many other contributing factors brought my inner spirit down, such as work coming before my wellbeing, misunderstandings in relationships, and no family or personal quality time. There were so many 'oughts', 'musts' and 'shoulds' flying around the place that it made me feel burdened – a burden that I felt was mine alone and therefore I was not free to share it in a way that perhaps would have relieved my burden.

Unfortunately, for a considerable time I carried all sorts of deep inner disappointments that had the ability to infect everything around and within me, all because of not talking honestly about what was truly bothering me. But thanks be to God, who I believe brought about a turning point (particular through my reading a book called *Putting Away Childish Things* by David A. Seamands). I can only say that the subject of the book spoke right into my tired and confused heart; I even felt that the author literally spoke about and to me. It was 'spot on' and very liberating to my mind and spirit. As I grew in spiritual wisdom and understanding, I was at last able to begin to open up my boatload of trouble with others.

This God-groundbreaking revelation came simply through verses from the Bible that seemed to radiate from the pages of the book I was reading. The irony of these 'shining' verses was that I had read them many times before but never discovered a meaningful personal connection to them. I should not have been surprised as to the power of the word of God, as it had a habit to speak truth into my life when I least expected it!

It was a relief to understand what I believe was God's view on the situation. God's words made it absolutely clear that the truth was to *set me free:* free to learn to be a God-pleaser rather than a people-pleaser; free to depend on him rather than do it myself; free to believe that I cannot have a negative mind and live at the same time positively in the ways of God. Thus, the verses that particularly moved me are as follows:

When I was a child, I talked like a child, I thought like a child, I reasoned like a child. When I became a man [or a woman], I put childish ways behind me.

1 Corinthians 13:11

Then we [I] will no longer be infants/children [of the past] tossed back and forth by the waves and blown here and there by every wind of teaching and by cunning and craftiness of men in their deceitful scheming. Instead, speaking the truth in love, we [I] will in all things grow up into him who is the head, that is, Christ.

Ephesians 4:14,15

For this reason, I remind you to fan [don't give up] into flame the gift of God [which is healing from damaged emotions] which is in you through laying on of hands [the work of the Holy Spirit]. For God did not give us [me] a spirit of timidity, but a spirit of power, of love, and of self-discipline.

2 Timothy 1:6,7

I came to understand that these biblical words spoke about my negative hang-ups that influenced, and even at time controlled and undervalued, my adult identity. The eye-opener for me was about receiving, and it enabled me to be set free from negative thought patterns that had influenced my present adult life. Consequently, these words brought me to a place of encouragement to persevere in living out my God-given identity; in other words, 'letting go' or 'putting off' or 'finishing with' the negative behaviour patterns and believing, studying and applying God's word in every situation. Of course, this did not mean that I never had a fall after that, but I did have an assurance that I was now going in the right direction – even though my circumstances took time to change.

In summary, as I look back I realise that it is easy to pray that God will change circumstances, but I have experienced that God is far more interested to bring changes in me. Therefore, I pressed on with determination to 'unwrap' and 'develop' God's gift to me of an abundant life.

I am aware that you too were going through a tough time while facing teenage years and that it was not always helpful to live in such an isolated area. But whatever our experiences, we came through them and I believe our lives were enhanced.

There is so much more I could write about these past years when we as a family lived in community, but this seems like a good point to stop for now.

I greet you with all my love
and remain always

Your Mum

Mother Britt

Tante Rösli   Muetti Hug you and me Mother Britt

Reflection

Time with Self

Lord, you know I very often pushed away
the child I do not want to be;
it filled with embarrassment the adult me
that made me sick, spoiled and humiliated.
Oh, I hated this voice wrestling in me!

But things changed, on a particular day as
I opened the window in my usual way
to the upward place, the heavenly realm;
I called it "time with God" – a good idea
to find my way back to where I belong, and
questioned him with issues I did not understand.

Selfishly I wondered whether today
he would hear and understand my ways:
"My God, where were you when I was born?
Why is it that my past looks down on me hurting and destroying?
Please, I pray, help, influence and change
the thought-pattern of my confusing early days."

Silently, I waited, sitting at his feet;
wondering... please... say something, I plead;
eventually, I was able to see the vision true
as I journeyed with my hand in his...
and walking in his landscape clearly.

I stopped off at one spot in our stroll,
his whisper reached my inner soil,
his words assured me with his truth:
"I am your creator God,
I saw you when you were formed;
I know what's best, allow me please,
I'd like to help, I have the key;

I'd like to heal,
believe my love is real.

Please, invite my presence to your broken heart
No longer hide your world so dark;
step out into the open and
let my light shine,
be embraced and include your injured self.
Trust my landscape and walk in my ways!"

The vision gone, I closed the window,
my heart burned with a song fresh and new
of what was and is and what will be.
Praise be to my creator God for answering me.

Jesus, Your Presence is My Blessing

Jesus, your presence is my only hope;
Your presence is my blessing.
Take and use what you can find;
allow my life to be your home.
Clear up, I pray,
cluttered-up corners and drawers.
Make it all your space;
hold nothing back, except your riches.
I long for you to be in the right place in my life.
Place your name at my front door;
answer the bells and take the calls.
Use my eyes, feet and hands in ways you know are right.
Your presence is my blessing.
And... Lord,
don't forget to reveal yourself to my neighbours.
And... I pray,
  be the central focus in my marriage,
  express your love where mine is failing.
  Your presence is my only hope;
  your presence is my blessing.
  I thank you. Amen!

LETTER 8

"I will listen to what God the Lord will say;
he promises peace to his people,
his saints – but let them not return to folly"

Psalm 85:8

Persevering – Past and Future

Don't ever give up...

Dearest Helen,

Through the media, I read that when Winston Churchill once was asked in an interview what experience had best equipped him to deal with his enemy (Hitler) leading up to and during the Second World War, he answered that he thought it might have been the time he had to repeat a grade in elementary school.

"You mean you failed a year in grade school?" the reporter asked disbelievingly.

Churchill responded indignantly, "I never failed anything in my life. I was always given a second opportunity to get it right."

Although I am in no way a Winston Churchill, I am able to identify with his reply because my experiences remind me of the many times when I did not get it right the first time or second and even beyond. Winston Churchill's issues were different from mine but nevertheless the same principle applies: don't give in when you miss the mark, but try again. So whatever went wrong, or whenever I missed a mark, it usually served to help me get it right the next time, which reflects what Winston Churchill was saying to the interviewer.

The repetition of opportunity served me well, as with hindsight it added strength and perseverance to my character. It also has been a tremendous help that I have never had the desire to dwell on 'failure' but rather to rise to the challenge of seeking a way through. I did this by clinging to my goal, namely, learning to live as God had planned. From experience, I knew that one of the ways to discover God's blueprint for successful and positive living is the reading and studying of his word, and believing and obeying what it teaches. I don't think that I exaggerate when I state that God's word seemed to have an answer for my every need. But of course, the other side of the coin is that changes in my life did not just happen overnight.

Let me give you some examples from when we lived in the Christian community[14].

When we first moved, I thought that the move would offer us a better life. My hope was that being with other Christians, we as a couple would no longer be living in our own little world, wondering what to say next or how to deal with each other's conflicts. I hoped that this new way of living and working with others would bring a fresh dimension into our marriage relationship. Unfortunately, this was not the case; if anything, it made our being together worse. We experienced lengthy seasons of frustration and strain, accompanied by many other factors that together made our togetherness at times extremely unbearable. We continuously lived in disharmony within our four walls, while to the outside world we pretended that all was well. And yes, we both seemed to be successful in helping and working for others, but our relationship stagnated in the background. I became particularly aware of a rising guilt of not meeting others' expectations of me as a Christian wife. I simply could not find the real answer to solve the issue even though I prayed and prayed...

Thankfully, this breakdown in our relationship eventually served me to be open about it and seek real help. God answered my prayers by sending two Bible-believing friends. As a result, the three of us came regularly together to pray and to ask God to bring insight as to why my life appeared to be so negative. We followed Jesus' advice:

> *Ask and it will be given to you; seek and you will find; knock and the door will be open to you. For everyone who asks receives; he who seeks will find; and to him who knocks the door will be opened.*
>
> *Matthew 7:7,8*

Through discussion and prayer, we did in fact receive some understanding regarding the existing situation that took us by surprise. Furthermore, the surprise was revealed through a traumatic personal and physical experience that happened the following way:

---

[14] Letter 7

One day while we were praying, I suddenly started to feel physically sick and went through the motions of heaving and throwing up from my inner being. As I did this, I repeatedly cried out, "I am ashamed... I am ashamed..." It was embarrassing the way I had to behave physically but we accepted it, and sure enough, the understanding followed in that the three of us believed that a deep-lodged 'root of shame' had been dislodged and brought out to be seen.

Early next morning, I was unwell. The doctor had to be called, who admitted me to the hospital. There they diagnosed stomach bleeding, to which appropriate treatment was given before I could return home in a couple of days. Now, was this stomach bleeding a coincidence or was it part of the ordeal while we were at prayer the day before? And what had it to do with my personal relationship with your dad? Not all the answers were clear at the time, and I still don't understand this completely, but from that day forth I experienced an inner lightness and wellbeing, even though life continued in the same place and with the same relationships. Without doubt, the experience influenced my attitude towards myself, others and God, and on top of everything else, it supplied me with a new energy to depend on and seek God.

One of the results of seeking God's guidance with my friends was that I deliberately started taking regular time out for reading and meditating on God's word. I began to realise that the more the word of God would occupy my mind, the better I would identify his voice and as a consequence would seek to follow his way rather than my own or other people's. Hence the psalmist's experience (Psalm 85:8 as quoted at the start of this letter) became part of my life's discipline as I realised afresh that peace, joy and stability were a result of trusting God even in situations I did not always understand.

In practice, time with God meant that I made the decision to organise my diary in such a way that allowed me periodically to retreat to a Church of England convent. And thankfully, your dad encouraged me to go, as it gave him his much-needed space. It also provided me with a space to be alone for reflections, unhindered prayers and the much-needed guidance for the practical outworking of my faith. So once a month I would arrive at the convent in the early morning and leave at 7pm. On other occasions I would stay for two to seven days.

Then once a year I would take time out for ten days, which was usually at the beginning of the year. I got into a habit of saying that I was "holidaying" with God because he was my focus and the Bible was my map.

In addition, I had the privilege while being at the convent of seeing the same nun, who on a daily basis met me for one hour to discuss what was going on in my physical and spiritual life. Her listening was well-focused and her words of response were always directed towards God. She would very graciously dwell on and question how God might view a situation, and for me this was just what I needed – always challenging but also encouraging.

At the end of each session the sister would close in prayer and issue me Bible readings and questions for reflection and application during the next 24 hours, as follows. I had to rise early and join the community for Morning Prayer and Holy Communion followed by returning to my retreat unit where I had breakfast. A very simple lunch and supper were available daily at a set time in a public room. The rest of the time was either spent in my room or in the chapel, and occasionally outdoors but always in an attitude of being in God's presence, listening, speaking and writing as the Spirit of God influenced my mind and spoke to me. I kept a detailed, honest journal of what I perceived throughout the day, including the thoughts and dreams of the night.

These 'away days' acted like a sieve that separated the wheat from the chaff, or where I was prompted to dig out the weeds that were growing and taking up some valuable space in my life's garden. For example, on one occasion the sister remarked that she had noticed changes in me but also added that she sensed that I harboured resentment (unconsciously) towards my husband. Her comment shocked me, but on personal examination of my heart, I recognised a problem and it also reminded me of the experience I had had whilst praying with my friends some while ago. Hence, in a repentant mood, I agreed. "Yes. I feel painfully trapped as a wife." Then I explained to her why and that I did not see a way out of the situation; on our wedding day I had promised to be married "for better or for worse" and this led me to endure my situation. Together we discussed my marriage relationship – how and why I had come to feel trapped, and how resentment had come to play a destructive role in our relationship. As we talked this over, light started to dawn; we discovered that my married life was fuelling scars of rejection and resentment from my past. Thus, the sister and I (with God's help) explored further how and why these emotions had had the opportunity to develop. As we continued talking, it became apparent that I had a great dislike for people who I felt were exercising control over me, which habitually made me feel insignificant. Although I had no problem recognising this as a tender, painful feeling that easily surfaced in certain circumstances, I had just accepted it. In summary, we came to a partial conclusion that resentment was part of my programmed emotional make-up and that my husband and the community in which we lived, unaware of my personality, had a habit of needing to be in charge of me and letting me know of their expectations.

Looking back on those years, it seemed that my life was more about those people and how to please them, and therefore the old scars were being scratched, bled and dressed up with artificialities. For example, I often felt chastised and belittled in my marriage, which in turn made me feel powerless and with no apparent breakthrough. I disliked these emotions intently.

It was so releasing to talk about it all and I was pleasantly surprised how God used and spoke to me through this loving and wise convent sister. As we came to the end of our one-to-one discussion, she spontaneously invited me to do the following exercises in my own time.

The first was to picture my husband in front of me, with me telling him of my resentments as forcefully as I could. And as I began to do this, I experienced total blankness and coldness which made me feel very uncomfortable. For the life of me, I could not find the necessary words to express myself. Quite incredible! But eventually, words and sentences began to form, and I wrote down on paper what I resented. The list was long. What an exercise! Remarkably, when I finished writing I experienced a deep sense of relief, but at the same time I felt guilty for having harboured such judgemental thoughts. I was further advised to reverse the role in my imagination by taking my husband's place, allowing him to reply to my 'resentments' and listen to his responses. This was equally astonishing and revealing – to see and hear how my behaviour affected him. But I also discovered how negative and uncertain he felt in our relationship. Then I was directed to imagine Jesus on the cross and to take all the time to picture him in vivid detail. When that was done, I had to travel back to the scenes of my resentments and stay with them for a while, then return back to Jesus crucified and gaze on him... In other words, I was encouraged to alternate between events that caused resentment and the scene of Jesus on the cross until I noticed the resentment slipping away from me, as I gave permission to Jesus to forgive me. It was all truly helpful in that I consciously 'let go' of all that had been, and in exchange I received an inner freedom of joy and light-heartedness.

In conclusion, the dear sister gave me some further advice to apply in the future: "Do not be surprised if the resentful feelings return after a while. Keep dealing with them patiently. Renounce negative feelings and replace them with the truth of the cross. Learn to neutralise your expectations of your husband and realise that he is under no obligation to live up to your expectations; they are yours and not necessarily his."

I am so conscious that life is full of *unlearning* while I am learning! The two, no doubt, go hand-in-hand. Being free from something does not necessarily mean that it will never turn up again but rather that I have learned a different way of dealing with it until it finally leaves me alone. This is good news!

I persevered applying God's truth when I was landed in questionable situations, and I learned that my expectations of my husband, whatever they were, had nothing to do with my genuine love being expressed to him; thus, I embraced my marriage vow, "till death us do part", with a fresh and meaningful gladness. I was also very conscious that God was clearly holding my life in his hands while I endeavoured to listen and seek to apply his words in all circumstances of my life.

James in his letter expresses it so well in what he is saying: that if we are doers of God's word, we will be blessed[15]; and Jesus encourages me in the same way:

---

[15] See James 1:25

Now that you know these things, you will be blessed if you do them...

So my experience has shown me that God knows so much better what is good for me and will give me what is appropriate for my growth as a whole person. Indeed, his provisions outweigh the world's handouts, in that he gives peace in turmoil, joy in sadness, stability in uncertainty, and so much more.

Our marriage relationship wonderfully took on a new meaning, for which I thank the Lord and the friends that stood by me.

As you know, some years later, when you were already well established with your life in Switzerland, your dad became terminally ill. Many of the things I had learned equipped me to accompany him faithfully and willingly to the very end of our time together. And what a privilege it was to stand by him through thick and thin – but I will write about this more in another letter.

How shall I round this letter off, then?

Well, God's calling on my life will never change but I will continue to be going through changes all the time. He is pleased when I walk in his way and I am content under his care, as I believe that in acceptance lies peace.

Mother Teresa's (1910-1997) life's motivation was exemplary and one that I truly desire to embrace:

> *He [Jesus] is the Life I want to live. He is the Light I want to radiate; he is the Way to the Father. He is the Love with which I want to love, he is Joy I want to share, he is Peace I want to show, Jesus is everything to me. Without him I can do nothing.*

Praise God!

I love you,

Your Mum

Reflection

I will listen to what God the LORD will say; he promises peace to his people, his saints – but let them not return to folly.

Psalm 85:8

I wrote the following verses quite a while ago. In them I am seeking to express my commitment to what I sense God would like me to hear and put into practice:

I will listen to what God the Lord will say;
Listen when my thoughts go astray,
His counsel I carefully observe
And cling to the truth, faithfully revealed through his word.

I will listen to what God the Lord will say;
Surrender my thoughts to his will each day,
Seek not to hinder the Spirit's work,
But trust and obey even if it hurts.

I will listen to what God the Lord will say;
He corrects, redirects, renews and sustains,
His will shall be completed, for this I am sure,
He is faithful, eternal, loving and true.

I will listen to what God the Lord will say;
To folly I will not return but seek his way,
As sure as the sun rises in the east
His light, his life and truth I will seek.

Now to Him who is able to do immeasurably more than all we ask or imagine, according to His power that is at work within us, to Him be glory in the church and in Christ Jesus throughout all generations, forever and ever! Amen!

Ephesians 3:20-21

LETTER 9

"The secret of change is to focus
all your energy, not on fighting the old,
but on building the new..."

This quote was written hundreds of years ago
by Socrates, a Greek philosopher, born in Athens
circa 470 BC.

Autumn Leaves – New Things to Come

Morning will arrive...

Dear daughter,

This letter is primarily about an experience in which I had to let go of something in order to receive something unknown in its place – a transaction that included heartache because what had to go was dear and precious. By nature, I would rather stick to the known than pursue the unknown, because the unknown has a habit of showering insecurity and this is not a comfortable feeling. Some of the definitions of 'letting go' (according to Google) are:

- relax one's hold (on);
- release, unhand, surrender or stop holding something;
- relinquish one's grip on someone or something;
- be willing to allow life to carry you to a new place, even a deeper, truer rendering of self.

I also came across the quote of Socrates at the start of this letter. I like it because it 'rings true' regarding some of my former experiences. I have included it in the hope that you too find his words inspiring during your seasons of change. The aspect that stirred me from this quote was that there is no gain in fighting, nor in hiding away the old, nor is there any advantage in ignoring inevitable changes; rather, we need to concentrate on building the new...

And so a situation arrived in which I had to discipline myself by focusing on building the new. After your A-levels at Henley College you chose to be trained for two years as a nanny at the Chiltern Nursery Training College (CNTC) rather than take the path to university, because you saw it best to learn something practical that would most likely offer you a job in the future. This also meant that you were disregarding society's expectations in order to follow your own path. I admired you for your courage and confidence!

In addition, after your schooling as a nanny, we as a family went through changes which affected us each in different ways. For you, you decided to go for your first job as a nanny to Switzerland, primarily, I think, because you wanted a taste of your mother's home country! Therefore, the CNTC helped and negotiated a job for you with a family with baby twins who lived by lake Zurich. Much had to be prepared before you could leave your parents' home, the place from which you had grown from a baby to a child, to a teenager, and now to a grown-up daughter who was ready to become an independent young lady with a job abroad. Wow, what a prospect!

Of course, I was delighted at the thought of you going to the place where I had been born and grew up. It made me feel proud that you felt daring enough to leave behind that which was familiar in order to take up the challenge of new things: being in a foreign land, having to learn a new language and having to live in an unknown household.

Despite my sense of pride, however, the thought of you leaving our home also made me sad. A picture surfaced in my mind of a fledgling bird flying out of its mother's nest to test out its own wings in order to begin to sustain its future life. The focus for me in this picture was not the bird but rather its wings. I accepted that you had arrived at your own 'moment', and just like the bird on the edge of the nest as it anticipates 'letting go', you too needed the space and time to test your wings so that you could develop your individual lifestyle and grow into a valued working member of this big wide world. But understandably, the mother in me preferred to cling and nurse the old and did not desire to let you go.

Ultimately, deep within, I knew the time had come for you to fly to a place of your own. So the whole episode of you leaving home became a learning curve for me. It was not just about a bird leaving its nest; this was a much deeper, poignant journey that I had to face and come to terms with in the coming weeks. I must admit that my attitude at the time was somewhat selfish, but I was acutely aware that your departure would literally bring lasting changes to our family set-up. I feared this change and I could hardly think of it without tears.

My list of 'moans' about life without you was huge. For instance:

- It was a painful thought that I would not be able see you any more in the way I was used to. Your everyday coming and going would become a memory from the past. How awful!

- Cooking and washing would be for one less person, meaning that I would miss you every time I cooked.
- I would not see your friends turning up anymore...
- There would be no daily hugs, no rubbing shoulders with you or grumbling and disagreeing; no discussing how to put the world right; no laughter, no compliments, no cups of tea and chatting over breakfast; no watching telly and crying together over programmes that touched our hearts.
- There would be no smiling face to greet me – your smile always reminded me of sunshine. Now this delightful sunshine would soon to be shining somewhere else.
- And there would be no waiting up for you...

It all sounded so sad! So in my heart, I harboured an sense of uncertainty as to how my life would turn out without your physical presence, and the thought of separation was a painful one. It concretely felt like I would be 'letting go' of what was dear and precious to me: you, my daughter.

My mind was filled with anxiety as I contemplated an unknown future. Your dad's attitude concerning these changes, in contrast, appeared rather pragmatic. He expressed little sentiment, and this only contributed to my low feelings. Furthermore, the thought of winter soon approaching with its long, dark days was also unhelpful.

I felt like a tree in winter time! The tree at one time had basked in spring and summer glory, and later in the autumn had changed into glittering and beautiful autumn colours – but then followed the sudden stripping of every leaf the tree owned as the weather turned cold, wet, dismal and windy. This image portrayed a very vivid picture of my own soul as I contemplated having to let go of your company, my beautiful and lovely daughter.

These emotions are of course necessary in order to appreciate more fully what is to come. The colder the winter, the better the spring; every tulip bulb needs the winter in order to bloom in the spring and so it is the wisdom of nature that living through the winter gifts us with the joy of spring. It was no different for me. My winter experience would soon change into spring, *praise be to our creator God!*

However, when New Year's Eve arrived, my thoughts were preoccupied with your forthcoming departure on 8th January. It was your last chance to celebrate with your friends, which you did, but I missed you on that night not being at home. To distract myself, I wrote a few meditative verses that passed through my thoughts that night. I called my verses...

The Challenge of a Goodbye

New Year has come, silent and swift;
alone I enter the New Day.
Downstairs on the settee, my husband,
he is sound asleep and at peace,
unaware of the arrival of another year.

New Year has come, no daughter at home;
far gone,
occupied sweet,
with the things, she delights
to usher her New Year in,
while I'm missing her at home.

New Year has come, what will it bring
for you, my daughter
and for me?
Before long you have flown away and
in that parting is my cry.

New Year has come, who will fill the void,
heal the pain that separation brings,
the sleepless nights it creates?
How am I to celebrate the coming days?

New Year has come, where will it lead?
How do I give my "Yes" to what's ahead?
Discover strength when none is found,
let go of what I can no longer hold?

New Year has come, I pause and pray;
my solace is meeting with my God and
paying attention to what is being said:
"Behold, I am with you always,"
and, "Do not fear what lies ahead!"

New Year has come!
I answer now;
let go – move on,
progress in knowing
that each goodbye
brings new beginnings
to be welcomed and explored –
I am not alone!

Oh, daughter of mine,
I can't help but counsel you
on this morning light of the New Year.
Keep open wide your eyes
and let its beam of wisdom rule your life.
Do not be deceived by the culture of this world,
choose your heart and faith to be your guide,
desire the place that you know is for you
and – yes –
seek the pearl of greatest price;
it will truly beautify your life.

Eventually your time arrived and you flew to Switzerland. For the first three months you suffered enormously from home sickness, which in a strange way comforted me! But thankfully you settled down and enjoyed your work and the new-found friends. I recall you being appreciative that the parents of the twins also employed a housekeeper who did all the cooking and cleaning. It was also the place where you first met your future husband. And I always used to be made to feel very welcome to stay when visiting you. So a feeling of spring had arrived in my heart as I realised that I had not lost you, but that you would always remain my daughter.

Now it is time to close this letter and as I am a lover and collector of quotes, I will close with the following words:

When our ego is humbled and not obstructing, God's creative Spirit can often have freer play. Like the bare trees, it may be that we allow the glory to shine through at these times more purely than in our summer prosperity.

Maria Boulding; The Coming of God; SPCK (1982)

With much affection,

Your Mum

P.S. I discovered the following relevant quote in one of my late diaries. The theme fits this letter, and I like it!

Growth means change and change involves risk, stepping from the known to the unknown.

Reflection

Many years ago, I copied into my diary the following prayer which was written by Sister Joyce Rupp O.S.M., who expressed to me so meaningfully what nature is able to teach:

A Prayer for Autumn Day

<u>God of the seasons</u>,
there is time for everything;
there is a time for dying and a time for rising.
I need courage to enter into the transformation process.

<u>God of autumn</u>, the trees are saying goodbye to their green,
letting go of what has been.
I, too, have my moments of surrender,
with all their insecurity and risk.
Help me to let go when I need to do so.

<u>God of the fallen leaves</u>
lying in coloured patterns on the ground,
my life has its own patterns.
As I see the patterns of my own growth,
may I learn from them.

<u>God of misty days</u> and harvest moon nights,
there is always the dimension of mystery and wonder in my life.
I need to recognise your power-filled presence.
May I gain strength from this.

<u>God of orchards</u> and fields of ripened grain,
many gifts of growth lie within the season of my surrender.
I must wait for harvest in faith and hope.
Grant me patience when I do not see the blessings.

God of birds flying south for another season,
your wisdom enables me to know what needs to be left behind
and what needs to be carried into the future.
I need your insight and vision.

God of flowers touched with frost,
and windows wearing white designs,
may your love keep my heart from growing cold
in the empty seasons.

God of life, you love me,
you believe in me, you enrich me,
you entrust me with the freedom to choose life.
For all this I am grateful. Amen![16]

Sister Joyce Rupp

---

[16] Used by permission

LETTER 10

"I will give you the treasures of darkness,
riches stored in secret places,
so that you may know that I am the LORD,
The God of Israel, who summons you by name."

Isaiah 45:3,4 (emphasis added)

Hard Pressed – but Not Crushed

Hidden pearls...

To my dear daughter Helen,

Do you ever feel that when you had to leap over a life's hurdle, another inescapable obstacle appeared and with it renewed worries emerged? *How can I find strength to work through it?* Of course, we all have hurdles, no matter how big or small, that we must overcome in order to survive. No one is exempt and it is so true that at times the stormy weather seems to be endless.

For us, a tragedy arrived when we were harshly interrupted by your dad having his first stroke – at a time when we both had a sense of wellbeing, when he and I were peaceful and content together. The season of illness shocked and controlled our lives and it felt like our world had come to an end. Now looking back, in spite of the sadness and shadows that engulfed us at the time, we experienced amazing support. And so I decided to write down some of my experiences that I went through as I faced the changes that were taking place in your dad's life. My desire is to give you a balanced view of our heartfelt struggles and how we were helped through them.

I learned so much about the goodness of God at that time! This was often experienced through the actions of other people and various unexpected incidences that sustained and strengthened me to 'look up' rather than down. The Bible text I chose for the beginning of this letter is one God used to speak to me of optimism in turbulent times. He showed me that I could find treasures in dark places, that indeed had the power to illuminate my path. And yes, I understood that these treasures had already been stored up for me and were waiting to be revealed at the right time and in the right place by God my creator. I also came to understand that these treasures were not referring to material wealth that would, for example, buy me out of the situation, but rather to the promises of God Almighty. He would see me through each day as I put my trust in him. So I understand that the "riches stored in secret places" belong to God alone, who will distribute them or hand them out in his time as I trust him. And why? Well, the text exclaims, so that I may know that He is God. What a treasure I hold in every situation, having the opportunity to know God and the fact that God knows me.

Although I was not released from the hard circumstances, I was graciously led through to the other side. Perhaps, then, you can understand why my heart delights to be writing and passing on to you and others some of my story of God's faithfulness. He has truly made all the difference and enriched every situation. I am so proud to tell you that all I have needed, God's hand has provided.

At the beginning of 2003 your dad had his second and more serious stroke; a real situation that we could not escape. Looking back, it all felt like a heavy stone that landed in our garden of life that was too heavy to move. It seemed to announce, "I am here to stay!" As a result of your dad's stroke, he was paralysed on the left side of his body, which included his left chest muscles and his swallowing tract. His speech was impaired but thankfully we could always understand what he was saying.

The outcome of his paralysed swallowing tract was that he was fed artificially via a tube that was operated into the abdominal wall leading directly into his stomach to receive his food. And so his twenty-four-hour professional care started. This care continued as he lay for months in a hospital bed before he was finally transferred to a nursing home.

You might well remember the beginning of these events. You were well settled in Switzerland but you arrived with your baby daughter Anna to view the situation for yourself. What a treat your arrival was to me in the midst of calamity! Obviously, your future visits were limited and therefore it was vital that we could share through letter-writing and phone calls, as we had no connection to the internet in those days. This motivated me to persevere with writing my diary which, as I remarked before, proved to become a secret way of working out with God what was going on in my thoughts. Yes, my diary-writing was a wonderful and personal way of communication and reflection through which I often discovered God's point of view on a situation.

Oh, your poor dad... It was a very hard time for him. His long stay in the local hospital did not ease his situation and was a trial in every way imaginable. The hospital authority was slow in moving him to a nursing home, as his life expectancy was a maximum of one year.

But with time we learned that our Lord God had a different view on his life. We were blessed with friends who supported us financially which enabled your dad to finally be transferred to a private nursing home. What a humbling experience, being supported financially, but nevertheless we received it with gratitude.

The move to the nursing home happened at the beginning of the autumn season, and our first Christmas with the staff at the nursing home turned out to be a memorable experience that was wrapped in both sadness and joy.

We had been married for thirty years so it was strange for me to be alone in our home. Remember, we usually started our family Christmas on Christmas Eve, but not this year! Understandably my mood was one of loneliness mixed with disorientation and a cloud-like sadness as I viewed the coming celebration days. How would each of us cope? What would Christmas Day be like in a nursing home?

I did not decorate our house as was my usual practice – to do so seemed pointless. But I did not dwell too long on what made me sad. Instead, I followed a nudging thought from within my heart to look for the star that I remember was among our Christmas decorations upstairs. *Be positive,* I said to myself. I put up the large star in our front window for every passer-by to see; an expression of my conviction that our home, including the nursing home, could acknowledge that it was Jesus' birthday!

Did I not believe that he could be found and celebrated anywhere? Had I not learned that God in the person of Jesus could use every event in our lives for good? Yes, indeed! I felt energised that we were celebrating the birth of Jesus – an event that gave me every reason to be thankful in the here and now. Consequently, I faced my day with gladness, purpose, courage and strength. I prayed, "Thank you, Lord! I welcome you into our home this Christmas and I continue to welcome you in my life. I pray that you, Jesus, will be seen and felt by everyone I meet on this day. And may my life be the fragrance of Jesus at the nursing home, in my husband's room and in reaching out to the nursing personnel. Amen!"

I now realise that this kind of experience was like finding a treasure in the dark, that shone out its light even though the darkness prevailed. Added to this, two different families from my neighbourhood turned up at my door with Christmas wishes for your dad and me. Through these people God expressed his love and concern and reminded me of the Christmas message: *God with us.*

I left my home at ten o'clock smiling and excited about the day. It was a long, tiring and somewhat strange day but it was satisfying, and I felt deeply sombre as I realised that life would never be the same again, even though your dad and I both continued to be fundamentally the same people. Later, as I entered my front door, the star that I had placed in the window in the morning encouraged my thinking, along with the words of a chorus:

All may change but Jesus never, glory to his name.

Thank you, Lord, for the pearl in the dark!

The next few days were uneventful, then New Year's Eve arrived, which was as challenging as Christmas Day. The weight on my shoulders felt heavy as I made my way up to bed because I could not help thinking about the future of our lives together yet living separately. The next morning, as I opened my eyes, it felt as if I had been thinking about the unknown future all night! Feeling too tired to get up, I lay in my bed dreaming, imagining and anxiously entertaining one thought after another:

- How would I cope with what lay ahead?
- How would your dad fit into his restricted life, long term?
- How would he cope being continuously washed and dressed?
- What about his swallowing problem? The physiotherapy treatments?
- Would he be learning to stand once again on his own two feet?
- If yes, would he be able to return and be cared for at home?
- What would the outcome be of all these real issues?

I also reflected on experiences your dad had already had, such as undergoing many moments of vulnerability and often feeling isolated because of being continuously cooped up in one room. He often verbalised that he felt like a prisoner in his own body, saying, with an awkward smile, "I am fit only for the dustbin."

Once, as we sat together in his room talking about our situation, we discussed that the Bible teaches us to call on God; he will hear and answer our prayers. Your dad replied, "He certainly does not seem to hear me, let alone answer my prayers."

These were heart-breaking moments on this New Year morn that could have easily dragged me down to a place where no room was found for hope. But thanks be to God that in his vocabulary 'hopelessness' does not exist! Of course I felt unsettled and discouraged, but my faith invited me, in the midst of gloom and doom, to choose life with God, to listen to his voice and to love his ways and hold fast. In other words, I was to cling to his promises and watch with expectancy God's goodness and love being worked out in our lives. My part was simply to trust and obey.

Let me close this letter by sharing the words of a poem written by Minnie Louise Haskins in 1908, which is the year your Swiss grandmother was born. Haskins was an American lecturer at the London School of Economics who wrote as a hobby, and this particular poem was a favourite of Queen Elizabeth, the late Queen Mother. When she showed it to her husband King George VI, he included it in his famous Christmas message broadcast in 1939 at the beginning of the Second World War. It is known that after the King's death, the Queen Mother had it engraved on bronze plaques on the entrance to the King George VI Memorial Chapel in Windsor. And just as this poem spoke in days of old, so it had maintained its power to speak and encourage me at this challenging time.

I said to the man who stood at the gate of the year,
"Give me a light that I may tread safely into the unknown."
And he replied,
"Go into the darkness and put your hand into the hand of God.
That shall be to you better than light and safer than a known way!"
So, I went forth and finding the Hand of God
Trod gladly into the night.
He led me towards the hills

And the breaking of day in the lone East.
So heart be still!
What need our human life to know
If God hath comprehension?
In all the dizzy strife of things
Both high and low,
God hideth his intention.

Minnie Louise Haskins (1875-1975)

With love,

Your Mum

Reflection

The following song became fixed in my heart and I used it when a solemn mood of desolation and fear of the future gripped me. At those times, out came the guitar! And with a childish enthusiasm and confidence I would sing the song as a prayer. As I sang and played, I dedicated all the worries of my heart to the Creator of my life. Never have I been let down by him. He is constant. Praise his name!

Eugene I. Clark wrote this song, *I Know Who Holds the Future* (1947). He was a songwriter and missionary who apparently wrote many meaningful songs.

I do not know what lies ahead,
The way I cannot see;
Yet One stands near to be my guide,
He'll show the way to me:

Chorus:
I know who holds the future;
And he'll guide me with his hand.
With God things don't just happen;
Everything by him is planned.
So as I face tomorrow,
With its problems large and small,
I'll trust the God of miracles,
Give to him my all.

I do not know how many days
Of life are mine to spend;
But One who knows and cares for me
Will see me to the end:
I know who holds the future...

I do not know the course ahead,
What joys and griefs are there;
But One is near who fully knows,

I'll trust his loving care:
I know who holds the future...[17]

Know that the Lord is God. It is he who made us, and we are
his; we are his people, the sheep of his pasture.

Psalm 100:3

The following is another quote that I pulled out of my collection, but I can't remember where I found it, except that it is said that these words were displayed in a shop window in America:

When we depend upon man, we get what men can do.
When we depend upon prayer, we get what God can do.

And so I have gradually come to understand that nothing is too great and nothing is too small to be committed to, and be managed by, the Lord God.

---

[17] © Song Solutions; used by permission

LETTER 11

"Your word is a lamp to my feet and
a light to my path."

Psalm 119:105
"By your words I can see where I am going,
your words throw a beam of light on my dark path." (MSG)

Thorny Days – Sunshine Encounters

Light on my path...

The Start of a Difficult Day

Life gets tedious.
Today
is far too much like
yesterday
and the day before yesterday,
and
the day before that.

I don't want to get on with the business
of living
today.
I know what jobs I've got to do
and I don't want to do them.

I know what people I've got to meet
and I don't want to meet them.
I know the places I've got to go to,
and I don't want to go there.

As I look at them,
the tiniest duties of the day
become enormous.

Today
I feel beaten before I start.

Did you ever feel like this,
Jesus?
That's funny!

As soon as I ask the question
something is different.

There's a shift in the perspective
of what is visible
as I look at today.

For now, I see that
today contains Christ.

He has become a part of this terrible day.
And the day is not terrible.

He has gone before.

Already he is present in the midst of
everything
that makes it dreary –
the dreariness begins to disappear.
It's as if the sun is beginning to shine.

My dear Helen,

I love the prayer that I included on the previous pages; it comes from my diary and I retrieved it years ago from a booklet that once was in my possession called *God's Thoughts*, by Dick Williams. Sadly, I can no longer find the book, nor do I know the poem's author. I remember, however, that I was impressed with the content of the prayer because I came across it when your dad had been in care for one year. And I felt in a similar situation to that of the writer, in that *my* days, too, were tedious and repetitive; I followed what was expected of me

I faced repeated problems with the care your dad received. Relationships with the nursing staff started to fall apart, and a time arrived when I did not want to face each day. I felt beaten and tired before the day even started. And this is why Dick Williams' prayer touched and challenged me as he expressed his feelings, thoughts and struggles.

So I followed his example and posed similar questions to Jesus: "Did you ever feel like this, Jesus? Did you ever, in your earthly life, feel depleted and at the end of your resources?" As I prayed and laid my challenges before the maker of heaven and earth, I realised once again that my supplications had been heard. Then my attitude towards my feelings and situation shifted and I recognised that I had been concentrating too much on myself and not enough on the presence of Jesus, who very clearly invited me to cast all my anxiety on him.

Why does Jesus invite us to do that? Because he cares. The psalmist says that God's word "is a lamp to my feet and a light to my path" and a similar exaltation later in the same psalm brought meaning and encouragement to my tired mind and heart in those days: "The unfolding of your words gives light; it gives understanding..."[18] *Great!*

I find it so interesting that the words I had been reading days or weeks ago suddenly became alive, shining and crying out with meaning for a particular situation. The memory is amazing!

Now, in this letter, I will tell a little more about the situation in those difficult and weary days. After the forecast of one year for your dad to live following his second stroke, he progressed very slowly into a

---

[18] Psalm 119:105,130

second year. However, there was no way he could be looked after at home. Therefore, a decision had to be made whether he was to be transferred from being a private patient to an NHS patient. Normally, the private nursing home did not keep NHS patients, and we had now reached the point when the funding for the private home had come to an end. But fortunately, God caused the manager of the home to examine our case very graciously and sympathetically. After long negotiations, the result was that your dad's monthly pension would contribute to his care and the NHS would make up the difference. The beauty of this was that his care could then continue in the same private home. We both looked on this as a very positive, helpful and encouraging result in these challenging times.

As for me, I had to learn to live in two places, which increasingly took over my life. Occasionally, I would take your dad out in his wheelchair for a smoke and a change of scenery. But it was hard work and demanded energy from me that dwindled as time went by. I experienced a period of intense tiredness, feeling that my own life was slipping away. Geographically and emotionally, I felt cornered and hemmed into a particular limited space, and on top of it all, I felt increasingly cut off from my normal life and friends. Even if I had a day off, I could not escape the pain of our situation, longing for a better time for us both. These feelings consumed me day and night, hour by hour – lingering, seeking, wishing, hoping for something like a magic wand that would vanish away these circumstances like in a fairy tale. But, of course, this could not happen! My wishful thinking was not the right way to moving forward in the situation, and if anything, it made me even more tired, disillusioned and grumpy!

As I mentioned previously, the turning point was when I read the prayer poem and Psalm 119. It was as simple as that: I turned away from self to Christ, my attitudes changed, and it made all the difference in facing my day.

I came to recognise that my duty to your father was no longer "I must" but a love gift. I *desired* to sit and be with him, feel what he felt, care for and support him, no matter what the cost involved. With time, he even allowed me to speak up for him when he felt that the staff did not understand him and had spoken *at* him rather than *with* him... Also, when I heard from different visitors that your dad had told them he would like me to know that he truly appreciated my commitment and care for him, this gave me great encouragement and was an incentive to carry on. In the past he had preferred not to praise me, his reason being so that I would not get proud! (This was probably his sense of humour.)

There were so many issues that came to the forefront that were delicate, difficult and required heart-searching. In all our ups and downs I had every reason for fostering thankfulness though, because support always seemed to arrive at the right time. Indeed, I found ever new reasons for joy and meaning in the midst of complicated demands. God's word guided, touched and quickened my weary feet at every corner, and how precious and real that experience was at times! I often prayed:

"Oh Lord, teach me to pray; teach me not to worry over things that I cannot change but instead motivate my spirit to trust you whatever the circumstances. Today, I give it all to you, every detail, every barb, every frustration, the major things and the petty things. May they all serve to draw me closer to you. Please, Lord, help me to nurture a Christ-centred daily spiritual life that looks outward instead of nursing self-interest. And grant me, I pray, grace to co-operate with what you see needs to be done so that you may receive all the praise. Thank you so much for reminding me of the truth that the grass withers and the flowers fade, but that your word stands forever. Thank you! Amen!"

As I come to the end of this letter, let me quote a line of an old hymn that emphasises the attitude I desire:

The storm may roar without me,
My heart may low be laid,
But God is round about me
And can I be dismayed?

This hymn, *In Heavenly Love Abiding*, has been much-loved and sung down the ages, and even to this day. It was written by a poet and hymn-writer, Miss Anna Laetitia Waring (1820-1910). And from the website *Stem Publishing* I gleaned the following:

She was born in 1820 at Neath in Glamorganshire, South Wales, where it seems she spent her whole life. It has been said of her, "Few authors are so sensitive or shy of publicity as Miss Waring. She has written her heart into her hymns, but particulars of her life and education are concealed from us." She was the daughter of Elijah Waring and niece of Samuel Miller Waring.

I was fascinated by the fact that her name and birthplace (Neath) also belong to your father's family; our late English grandmother was called Waring before she married your granddad. The whole family came from Neath, just as this hymn-writer did. So inquisitively I asked myself, was this hymn-writer a relative of your father's family? Even though I did not find an answer to my questions, I found these links fascinating and interesting. I vividly remember the many visits your dad and I made to Neath, visiting the Waring family before we were married, and later with you. Interesting, is it not?

Thank you, my daughter, for bearing with me and taking time to read all these events of my life. As a final item, I have enclosed verses that I myself put together that simply express some of my inner thoughts. I hope you like them. Enjoy!

With lots of love
and I'll be always

Your Mum

My Heart is a Garden

The path I tread reflects my life
In surface and in slope
Though stones and gravel make it hard
They never dim my hope.

My hope that lawns of camomile
And other scent so sweet
Will keep me true to God's desire
And guide me till we meet

So as the seasons come and go
My paths will twist and turn
To live my life as God has planned
His footsteps I must learn

Lead me to a better place
Allow my eyes to see
The creation, God, that you have given
To all the World and me.

The hidden life ....

Resurrection

Natural process

darkness · light
life · death
up · down
in · out

RAIN + SUNSHINE

air · caring environment

Blossom

Joy of oneness

wholeness

OPENING up

Violet

LIFE - eternal newness

Colours

Fruit

sight ·

sound

BEAUTY

celebration

life out of ...

Alive · abandonment
of self to God

STIRRINGS OF LIFE

Waking up

Pushing out

Sprouting

GOD BROKE Through

BREAK THROUGH
of newness

Stillness

In the darkness of
soil the seed ge...

Stillness

New pote...

DARK CHRIST

agony

Space

rejection

Bulb, seed, bud contains

Longing

Hope

Growth

Courage

SEEKING

LONELY

waiting

Death

Burial

Weak

rot

DEATH

LIVE

Cold

Expectations

love

Hopeless

the full beauty

bright

Grief

silence

Brokenness ...

Bareness

Root deve...

me...

for suppo...

un hurried

fear

Soil of my life · God's joy love + life is waiting here to be expressed up th...

145

Reflection

I love to observe nature because what I see there often reflects the experiences of life. It has been my habit to collect quotes, verses etc. because their words so often express what I have needed to be challenged with as I have faced particular circumstances.

My chosen verses for this page are called *Planted*. The poem symbolises to me the principle that roots must be established first before satisfactory growth can be seen above the ground. I have repeatedly observed this in my experience of gardening, whether it was a tree, shrub or plant; the upward growth would always look unhealthy if a root problem existed. Something else I have learned is that no tree or plant can be expected to thrive if it is forever being transplanted. Horticultural knowledge tells me that it is the root that supports the tree, or shrub, or plant, and not the other way around. And so in an uncomplicated way, I love to see my earthly life as being rooted in the soil of God's word. It is this that has nurtured and supported my life to this very day.

> *By your words I can see where I am going,*
> *your words throw a beam of light on my dark path.*
>
> Psalm 119:105 (MSG)

In the midst of his sorrow Job said:

> *"I have not departed from the commands of God's lips; I*
> *have treasured the words of his mouth more than my daily*
> *bread."*
>
> Job 23:12

God the creator was Job's gardener too and his 'life roots' established in God's word sustained him, like me through the storms of life.

Planted

You shall take root downward,
and bear fruit upward.
Yes, as your roots;
so, your fruits;
from me is your fruit found.

As your roots go deep in the ground
of my life,
as you draw from me
all that your soul needs,
for activity, health, liberty,
a life outpoured in fruitfulness,
so, shall this come about.

You are planted
on the soil of my word,
that your soul may be
nourished by the word.
Yes, you are planted
in the land of promise,
that each promise may be yours.

Yes, you are planted
in the likeness of death,
that you may bear
his resurrection life.
He seeks in you
an abundant harvest.
He gives to you
the early and the latter rain.
He watches over you,
he rejoices with you...

Author unknown

LETTER 12

"Strength of my heart, I need not fail,
Not mind to fear but to obey,
With such a leader, who could quail?
Thou art as thou wert yesterday.
Strength of my heart, I rest in thee.
Fulfil Thy purposes through me."

Amy Carmichael (1867-1951)

Serving – Choices to Make

Taste and see...

Dearest daughter,

Do you remember when you broke your elbow while stepping outside your home to reach your rubbish bin? The news came as quite a surprise to us. And then later we heard that the X-ray showed that you had broken the radial head just below your elbow. As there was significant damage to the elbow joint, surgery was required to pin the broken bones together.

Your family clearly needed help while you were in this unfortunate position since your arm had to rest in order to heal, and I was delighted to be asked to come and be of assistance. But as you know, I hesitated at first, as I was reluctant to leave your dad. Eventually, however, I decided (as did everyone around me) that your needs were greater than his, as he was being cared for by the nursing staff. I did not waste much time then but booked my flight with enthusiasm. I was so looking forward to seeing you all and also to having a change of scenery.

You were still in hospital following my arrival, and it was quite extraordinary what took place over the next forty-eight hours. The situation in your household grew worse as Anna developed a severe stomach upset during the night and had to be admitted to hospital. Her dad accompanied her and took charge of her situation while I stayed back to care for your four-month-old baby, Evan. It was a very difficult time for me, as I found myself alone in the house with Evan, trying to properly look after him and organise his feeds. It gave me a headache at first, but then I sought help from a neighbour who was able to give some instructions. What fun! But despite the challenges, it drew us all closer together and I started to enjoy being of use in a totally different way.

Eventually everything settled back into a more normal way of life. You came back home as a mother and wife, but with only one hand and arm in action. Anna recovered, your husband returned to work part time and you received a home-help who made her contribution in supporting you wherever you needed it most.

My stay lasted for two-and-a-half weeks before I returned home. And although it was an unexpected visit, I enjoyed myself thoroughly in being with you. In fact, the thought of returning to the situation back at the nursing home felt somewhat depressing. But I knew and accepted that this was the right place for me; once home, I reminded myself that I was called to be a blessing and support to your dad, and to be an expression of unconditional love in thought and action.

Wonderfully, significant words from the Bible kept coming back to memory – things I had previously learned by heart:

> *The LORD gives strength to his people;*
> *the LORD blesses his people with peace.*
>
> Psalm 29:11

> *"Therefore, do not worry about tomorrow, for tomorrow will worry about itself. Each day has enough trouble of its own."*
>
> Matthew 6:34

Unquestionably I was hanging on to the promises of God's strength and his blessings. I comforted myself in the belief that Jesus knew what was in my heart. He knew my likes and dislikes, what I was thinking, and that I was sometimes critical of people around me. He also knew that at times I was thinking nothing! – and at other moments my thoughts and motives led me to looking better on the outside than the inside. But in it all, I simply believed that help was at hand as I faced my weaknesses honestly. I accepted what I could not change, for the time being. And so I prayed:

"Lord, continue to help me to watch over my thoughts and speech. Grant me wisdom to apply your word in my daily living. Thank you for forgiveness when I am going astray in thought, word and deed. Thank you, Father God, that I have been given the opportunity to serve my daughter and her family in their needs. And now I thank you afresh that I am back with my husband to serve him with determination and your strength. Thank you, Jesus, that you are the perfect example of giving, and of serving others. Grant me your Spirit and weave your life into mine so that I might daily make the right decisions and face each day with an undying purpose to serve. Amen!"

Once home, I surveyed my garden. This was my pride and joy; I always worked it with pleasure. Much had changed in it while I was away. *Wow* – there was work to be done and my fingers were itching to get stuck into it; but I chose, as soon as time allowed, to relax in my private place for stillness and to think through what was on my mind, rather than busy myself catching up on things in the house and garden. And as I did so, I was reminded of one of William H. Davies' (1871-1904) poems, called *Leisure* (1911).

What is this life if, full of care,
   we have no time to stand and stare.
No time to stand beneath the boughs
   and stare as long as sheep or cows.
No time to see, when woods we pass,
   where squirrels hide their nuts in grass.
No time to see, in broad daylight,
   streams full of stars, like skies at night.

Yes, it was so good that in the midst of concerns, and even anxieties, I chose first to do nothing but sit, stare and think – allowing myself to become focused on the tasks ahead.

It was with a thankful heart that I inspected the garden from one corner to the other, seeing how the pears on the tree had grown to a fair size. Some tomatoes were red; the beetroots had grown to an edible size; the leeks looked good; the lettuces and beans had all grown and were ready to be picked. What a feast it all presented with its fruitfulness before my eyes! I said to myself, "This is what God is looking for in my life: fruit that will be for enjoyment and to bless others." I also noted, "Think of it – I did the sowing of the seeds and the planting, then I went away and nature did the rest in providing rain, air and sunshine, light and darkness and more." God gave me eyes to see and lips to praise; a sense of smell for the fragrance that circled the air; a mind that noticed the flowers bathing their petals in the warmth of the sun. I also could enjoy the sun and it stirred a response of love to a faithful God who provided it all.

My hearing was rewarded too by a soothing sound from my small water feature that reminded me unmistakably of Jesus' words:

> *"If anyone is thirsty, let him come to me and drink. Whoever believes in me, as the Scripture has said, streams of living water will flow from within him."*

John 7:37b,38

I was thirsty alright; therefore, I drank the words of Jesus to find refreshment for each day, allowing those words to apply to the situations around me and the turmoil within me, especially in the context of the nursing home.

As I continued to browse the landscape of my garden, I became more aware of the many different colours that were on display, all harmonised wonderfully together. There was a moment when I could not help spotting some flowers wilting, weeds had taken root, the lawn needed cutting. It all spoke volumes to me. What an amazing creation was displayed in my little garden! *Oh, how I love and adore the language of nature. Thank you, Lord God!*

In summary, it was not easy to pick up where I had left off when I returned from Switzerland. I could easily have allowed my heart to be filled with resentment and despair. But instead, I chose to be led and encouraged by my gardener God, to be still, to listen and to hear words of hope and love through his creation.

As I close this letter, I remind myself again that 'in acceptance lies peace'.

And so I am heartily yours,

Mum

Reflection

The poem below is by Hannah Hurnard (1905-1990), a Christian
author and best known for her allegory *Hinds' Feet on High Places*.

In acceptance lieth peace,
O my heart be still;
Let thy restless worries cease
And accept his will.
Though this test be not thy choice,
It is his – therefore rejoice.

In his plan there cannot be
Aught to make thee sad:
If this is his choice for thee,
Take it and be glad.
Make from it some lovely thing
To the glory of thy King.

Cease from sighs and murmuring,
Sing his loving grace,
This thing means thy furthering
To a wealthy place.
From thy fears he'll give release,
In acceptance lieth peace.

LETTER 13

"We are not made for mountains,
the sunrises,
Or for the other beautiful
attractions in life –
those are simply intended
to be moments of inspiration.
We are made for the valley
and the ordinary life
and that is where we have to prove
our stamina and strength."

Oswald Chambers (1874-1917)

Nursing Home – Paved with Humiliations

Strengthening roots...

Dear daughter,

Continuing on from my last letter, you might recall that my life now consisted of living in two places whilst carrying an increased desire and compassion to support your dad in his suffering. I noticed that from time to time my mind gave way to thoughts of either a speedy ending, or a quick recovery – neither of which were right of course. The following quote edged itself into my diary and I found that the truth of the words could easily be applied to me:

> *Most of us would prefer, however, to spend our time doing something that will get immediate results. We don't want to wait for God to resolve matters in his good time because his idea of 'good time' is seldom in sync with ours.*
>
> *Oswald Chambers (1874-1917)*

Even though the nursing home had its benefits, it was lacking in emotional and personal support. For example, a certain event that occurred involving one of the residents left a lasting impression. This encounter was an emotional experience that brought tears to my eyes – but I also learned from it. It energised me as I reflected back on the day while writing in my diary.

But first, let me give you a short introduction of what took place. The basic story was about Peter (not his real name) who was immobile and blind and whose room was opposite your dad's. Because of the proximity, we had got to know him and his wife fairly well. It was around evening mealtime on the day when Peter, after two weeks' holiday with his wife, was 'delivered' by the ambulance workforce, in his wheelchair and on his own, to the second-floor dining room. On his arrival, the evening meal was being served so it was a very busy time for the nursing staff. As usual, I was there helping with the meals, feeding patients and assisting with other small chores. Your dad was in his own room at the time since he was still unable to eat his food in the normal way.

Now that you have had the 'introduction', here is a piece of writing that I entitled *The Nursing Home.* It was a reflection of what took place and how I perceived what was going on among the lives of vulnerable, helpless and sick people, like Peter and your dad.

The Nursing Home

I touched Peter and said,
"It is nice to see you back from your holiday."
He sobbed for a moment or two –
he was away by the sea for two whole weeks
with a sweet group of people and
his faithful wife alongside him too.

He tried to eat the food set before him,
but neither hungry, nor able to see the meal,
the knife, the fork, not even the carers
who put the dish before him too –

He being blind – and still crying!

My heart went out to him,
sat by him for a while at the table,
put my hand on his for mutual understanding;
his tears moved me, I felt his pain
and plainly he was unable to say a word,
he felt misery to the core of his being
and unable to eat what he could not see.

I took his plate away and asked,
"Would you like a pudding?"
"Yes, please," he replied and so
I spooned the yogurt to his mouth
and I felt his thankfulness for what I was doing.

A carer came and stood by him,
administered the tablets and said,
"Take and swallow, they are for your own good."

No sympathy from the carer;
no time to stop and welcome him home;
too many chores like feeding others,
distributing the meals, drugs, telephone,
making drinks, answering calls
short staffed – stretched to her limits;
no wonder it was distressing to us all.

I pondered –
thankful that I took the time to see and listen to his
weeping.

I too had tears as I left the nursing home –
took time reflecting back over what had gone before.
Listened to my hurt and unhappy feelings,
wrote down on paper thoughts and their meaning.

Oh, nursing home, what a name,
daily I go in and out of that place of death,
visit my husband, who also is depending
so much on the kindness of 'the carers'
as he too is stuck like a bird in a cage,
but in spite of his limitations
is dreaming of the good old days and
hoping that one day his life will return
to what life was in his earlier days.

He is so brave!

At times I ask him, "How are you today?"
"Oh, not too bad," he replies.
At other times, his thumb is pointed down,
he whispers, "low" or "fed up" or "tired", "I've had enough."

He tells me frequently, "The carers have been rough,
they are always in a hurry when answering my bell,
they do not listen to what I say,
they disappear – I simply had to wait!"

It is a hard and a difficult situation,
a lonely road paved with humiliations.
It seems that everyone forgets that
he too is a man
who could once think and do things for himself.

And I, as his wife, at times feel so helpless,
tired of watching, waiting and crying –
widowed, yet I see my husband daily –

and so, my life too has taken on a different meaning,
struggling at times to accept the things I cannot change;
I too admit to feeling locked away in a corner
and patiently wait...
for a day... that says: no more.

At other times,
I wait for a sympathetic ear
that truly hears my pain
or a hand conveying some assistance
or an eye catching a glimpse of our sunken position
or even a prayer that indicates true care.

Oh, nursing home – our second home –
you demand a lifestyle we would never choose
and yet – it spells out a place of safety?

And so, at the end of my disturbing day,
life goes on and 'care' is given every day;
our carers' tasks are heavy and demanding;
they too have worries as strangers in this land.

Yes, we could easily do without this season;
and yet – this is what our life is about and
I do know that spring will follow after winter darkness
and suffering will eventually turn to bloom
with hope of new shoots sprouting.

Winter always passes when spring is about.
Our creator God is in charge of every season.
My heart comes to rest and strength abounds.
His views are best in every seasonal situation;
precisely, he always knows what's best.

Thanks be to God for our nursing home!

As I revealed my feelings through this poem, I felt an assurance that God never expected me to have to face more than I could bear. So the whole experience gave me a fresh understanding of the constant pressure that the staff were under in their pursuit of caring for the patients. As for me, the following became a source of strength to the core of my being: "I waited patiently for the Lord; He turned to me and heard my cry. He lifted me out of the slimy pit, out of the mud and mire; He set my feet on a rock and gave me a firm place to stand. He put a new song in my mouth, a hymn of praise to our God. Many will see and fear and put their trust in the Lord."[19] Wonderful!

Let me recall another delightful and comforting story written by another person who, like me, found a deep reward in times of need as he simply trusted Jesus. He taught me something of what prayer could mean to different people at different times in life. How and when this story slipped into my notebook I do not remember, nor do I have a record of its author, but I believe that it deserves to be passed on to the next generation:

---

[19] Psalm 40:1-3

The Chair

A man's daughter had asked the local minister to come and pray with her father. When the minister arrived, he found the man lying in bed with his head propped up on two pillows. An empty chair sat beside his bed. The minister assumed that the old fellow had been informed of his visit.

"I guess you were expecting me," he said.

"No, who are you?" said the father.

"I'm the new minister at your church," he replied. "When I saw the empty chair, I figured you knew I was going to show up."

"Oh yeah, the chair..." said the bedridden man. "Would you mind closing the door?"

Puzzled, the minister shut the door.

"I have never told anyone this, not even my daughter," said the man, "but all of my life I have never known how to pray. At church, I used to hear the pastor talk about prayer, but it went right over my head. I abandoned any attempt at prayer," the old man continued, "until one day about four years ago my best friend said to me, 'Joe, prayer is just a simple matter of having a conversation with Jesus. Here is what I suggest. Sit down in a chair; place an empty chair in front of you, and in faith see Jesus on the chair. It's not spooky because he promised, "I'll be with you always." Then just speak to him in the same way you're doing with me right now.' So I tried it and I've liked it so much that I do it a couple of hours every day. I'm careful though. If my daughter saw me talking to an empty chair, she'd either have a nervous breakdown or send me off to the funny farm."

The minister was deeply moved by the story and encouraged the old man to continue on the journey. Then he prayed with him, anointing him with oil, and returned to the church.

Two nights later, the daughter called to tell the minister that her dad had died that afternoon.

"Did he die in peace?" he asked.

"Yes, when I left the house about two o'clock, he called me over to his bedside, told me he loved me and kissed me on the cheek. When I got back from the store an hour later, I found him dead. But there was something strange about his death. Apparently, just before Dad died, he leaned over and rested his head on the chair beside the bed. What do you make of that?"

The minister wiped a tear from his eye and said, "I wish we could all go like that."

Ending this letter with
much love for you,

Your Mum

Reflection

Some quotes from my diary:

Lay before him [God] what is in us, not what ought to be in us.

C. S. Lewis

If we knew how to look at life through God's eyes, all life would become a sign. If we knew how to listen to God, all life would become a prayer.

Michel Quoist, Catholic priest (1918-1997)

To have faith in Christ means, of course, trying to do all that he says. There would be no sense in saying you trusted a person if you would not take his advice. Thus, if you have really handed yourself over to God, it must follow that you are trying to obey him. But trying in a new way, a less worried way. Not doing these things in order to be saved, but because he has begun to save you already. Not hoping to get to Heaven as a reward for your actions, but inevitably wanting to act in a certain way because a first faint gleam of Heaven is already inside you.

C. S. Lewis

One of my own prayers:

"Thank you, Lord God, that there is not one situation, however bad or sad, where you cannot come in with your Light. You are the Light of the World. Your Light gives life, your Light brings truth, your Light reveals to me what is important, and it brings your perspective on things. I truly thank you for being involved in my life, inspiring me, guiding me, illuminating darkness and uncertainties. And so I pray, go on indwelling me, expand yourself in me and radiate out to others your character. I thank you for the encouragement of today to accept what is and to trust you for what is to come. Amen!"

LETTER 14

"It is not our trust that keeps us,
but the God in whom we trust
who keeps us.
We have to pray with our eyes on God,
not on the difficulties."

Oswald Chambers (1874-1917)

In the Midst of Darkness –
Special Times

Not alone...

Dear Helen, my beautiful daughter,

I wrote in a previous letter about my visit to Switzerland when you broke your elbow. Now I am remembering another trip I made to see your family – such a positive and encouraging time.

I felt so relieved when your dad once again agreed for me to be able to spend time with you. He had been realising more and more that his body could no longer keep pace with his desire to come with me. It often saddened him – but I also should add that he was very brave in accepting his limitations. I admired the way he repeatedly expressed hope and the belief that he would one day have the chance to catch up on all the activities he was missing, which he had enjoyed in the past when he was healthy.

It brought a special closeness in our relationship to share these regrets and hopes that he expressed – but of course, we know that our clock cannot be turned back. So for our mutual well-being together, we discussed some important questions relevant to our situation:

- How do we handle our here and now together?
- What is it that brings comfort and encouragement into our lives?
- How do we aim to nurture a positive attitude in the midst of physical limitations?
- How can we continuously focus on our reality and be creative in every opportunity we have together?

All these questions were truly challenging but caused our lives to be more interesting on a daily basis.

But as I said, my aim for this letter is to reflect on my few days with you. One of the first things I must say is that your children were gorgeous and lively, and it gave me much pleasure being so near, to see them bubble over at the forthcoming Christmas. Nothing else seemed to be more important to them. As for you, I was aware that it was no easy task to be a mother of two and at the same time a wife and a daughter. On top of this you also needed to concentrate on the Christmas preparations. You had so much to do but with limited time and strength.

During the Christmas season our culture creates so much hassle and stress, when the opposite should be the case! For example, there is huge pressure to spend money even if money is not in our purses. If we are not careful, we are easily sucked into the commercialism of our time. However, I was pleased to notice that you had set boundaries on how much you allowed the building-up of Christmas to affect your family life, money and time; you did not give in to your children as they pushed you with determination about what they thought they would like to see under the Christmas tree. Oh, Helen, you are such an amazing mother, wife and daughter and it thrilled me to be part of the family at such a busy and challenging time.

All this and more gave me much to reminisce on as I travelled home after this special and meaningful time.

The weather on my return to the UK was frosty, misty and cold. The sun was darkened by clouds, creating a rather gloomy atmosphere and it probably will not surprise you that the weather reflected just how I was feeling as I re-entered my situation at the care home with your dad, to celebrate Christmas in entirely different surroundings from what I had just left behind. Days had passed since my return and I spent many hours sitting with your dad because of his physical weakness. Sadly, things for him had not changed. He still felt locked away in his room and he continued wanting to get better, but his support team did not see his health moving in that direction. If anything, his needs had become more intense, and I was not surprised, especially as his condition had entered its fourth year.

The battle to survive against all odds proved increasingly difficult and as a consequence, he felt very miserable and depressed, giving me a sense that his 'life candle' was shedding less and less light into his daily life. For example, this showed up in his sense of humour; whereas it had been so alive and brought cheer and laughter to so many visitors, it now seemed to be fading away. The atmosphere in his room could be compared to the forces of high winds blowing against him and exposing him to a rough existence with no escape or shelter, except death.

This brought a gloomy sense to life, even with Christmas at our door. I tried harder to encourage and support him, but it appeared to be to no avail. I so desperately wanted to do the best for him but eventually began questioning how much and how far I could accompany him on his journey. The most I could do was to keep praying and stay by him through thick and thin – and this I determined to do! Part of my inspiration to achieve this came from the words of a godly man known as Oswald Chambers, who was born in Aberdeen in 1874 and died in Cairo, Egypt in 1917. He was an early twentieth-century Scottish Baptist and a very influential theologian. He wrote many books on prayer and the Christian life and his writings have inspired many Christians down the years. His books are still sold and read today.

One of his most famous books that was influential to me was *My Utmost for His Highest*, which has been read all over the world and I have it on my bookshelf. The following quotes were helpful to me:

> *When we are abandoned to God, he works through us all the time.*

> *Prayer is to get hold of God, not of the answer.*

These words of encouragement inspired me to dwell on God's merciful ways and abandon to him my concerns, believing that he would act according to his will and in his time.

Another person who came to my mind at this time was a nun by the name of Mother Mary Clare. She said:

> *The essential heart of prayer is the throwing away of ourselves in complete self-oblation to God, so that he can do with us what he will.*

Although abandonment and self-oblation are very old words and their meanings could have negative influence on us today, I take it to mean that abandonment is letting God be God, letting him be in control and allowed to administer his way in my circumstances. This sounded consoling to my soul.

One of ways that your dad and I responded to our circumstances with a positive attitude was to prepare a present for each carer – fourteen of them! Our aim was to be generous and show our appreciation for all the hard work they were continuously doing for all the residents. Obviously, the bulk of the work in preparing these presents was done by me, but the project did provide a definite input into both of our lives. Your dad helped with the wrapping of each gift, and his highlight was signing each card with his own signature. What a signature he used to have before he became unwell – and was proud of it! I remember the big swing he used to make when he had to sign his full name on a document. In contrast now, it was a humbling experience for him and me to recognise that he could barely write his name. He did the best he could and he enjoyed doing it.

All the presents went into your dad's drawer and it was his task to hand them out to the individuals as they entered his room on Christmas Day and beyond. You can imagine how this simple activity was rewarding and satisfying, and showed me clearly that even the smallest spark of light could be used to good effect. God gave the gift of strength and ingenuity as we gave him our weaknesses and disillusionment. What more could we have asked? We rejoiced and were grateful for each moment we had together.

With anticipation, the celebration day arrived, and we gathered together, each one trying to be happy because that is expected in the culture we live. Even today, I can still hear the voices of the different carers saying, "Cheer up, it's Christmas." No one wanted to see a sad or gloomy face. Reaching the end of yet another Christmas Day, I felt absolutely exhausted but privileged to be sharing my life with the staff and residents alike. It was a very simple celebration, yet it was strangely satisfying, and what gave the day meaning for me was when, at the end, I asked myself the question, "Where would Jesus have chosen to celebrate his birthday – in the nursing home or at a rich man's table?" I know he has nothing against the "rich man's table" and neither have I, but for me it felt comforting and encouraging to believe that he would have preferred to mingle with the vulnerable, sick and lonely – of whom there were plenty in the nursing home. Even the life of Christ started in vulnerability and in a lonely place. And so I really considered myself honoured to be part of this community, and in some ways, I obtained a glimpse of what it means to let God influence our Christmas.

As I come to the end of this letter, I quote the following prayer that comes from my diary of that time. I have chosen to include it because the words are so poignant and relevant to me.

When the world was dark
and the city was quiet,
you came.

You crept in beside us.

And no one knew.
Only the few
who dared to believe
that God might do something different.

Will you do the same this Christmas, Lord?

Will you come into the darkness of today's world;
not the friendly darkness
as when sleep rescues us from tiredness,
but the fearful darkness,
in which people have stopped believing
that the war will end
or that food will come
or that a government will change
or that the church cares?

Will you come into that darkness
and do something different
to save your people from death and despair?

Will you come into the quietness of this city,
not the friendly quietness
as when lovers hold hands,

but the fearful silence when
the phone has not rung,
the letter has not come,
the friendly voice no longer speaks,
the doctor's face says it all.

Will you come into that darkness,
and do something different,
to embrace your people?
And will you come into the dark corners
and the quiet places of our lives?

We ask this because
the fullness we long for
depends on being open and vulnerable to you –
like you were to us,
when you came,
wearing no more than diapers,
and trusting human hands
to hold their maker.

Will you come into our lives,
if we open them to you
and do something different?
When the world was dark
and the city was quiet
you came.

You crept in beside us.
Do the same this Christmas, Lord,
Do the same this Christmas. Amen.[20]

---

[20] Reproduced by permission from *Cloth for the Cradle, Worship Resources and Readings for Advent, Christmas & Epiphany.* Copyright © 1997 WGRG, Iona Community, Glasgow, Scotland *wildgoose@wildgoose.scot; www.wildgoose.scot*

Lord Jesus, I thank you, that you have done this precisely for us, you crept in beside us. You spread your glow into our darkness and because of you we were able to shine out your light and be comforted.

Jesus said, "I am the light of the world. Whoever follows me will never walk in darkness, but will have the light of life."

John 8:12

Thank you, Lord!

I end this letter
with much thoughtfulness
for the here and now,

Your Mum

Reflection

One of the most beautiful of all Christmas stories was told by the American poet Edwin Markham (1852-1940), about a cobbler, a godly man who made shoes in the old days.

The Shoemaker's Dream

One night the cobbler dreamed that the next day Jesus was coming to visit him. The dream seemed so real that he got up very early next morning and hurried to the woods, where he gathered green boughs to decorate his shop for the arrival of so great a Guest.

He waited all morning, but to his disappointment, his shop remained quiet, except for an old man who limped up to the door asking to come in for a few minutes of warmth.

While the man was resting, the cobbler noticed that the old fellow's shoes were worn through. Touched, the cobbler took a new pair from his shelves and saw to it that the stranger was wearing them as he went on his way.

Throughout the afternoon the cobbler waited, but his only visitor was an elderly woman. He had seen her struggling under a heavy load of firewood, and he invited her, too, into his shop to rest. When he discovered that for two days she'd had nothing to eat, he saw to it that she had a nourishing meal before she went on her way.

As night began to fall, the cobbler heard a child crying outside his door. The child was lost and afraid. The cobbler went out, soothed the youngster's tears and, with the little hand in his, took the child home.

When he returned, the cobbler was sad. He was convinced that while he'd been away he had missed the visit of his Lord. Now he lived through the moments as he had imagined them: the knock, the latch lifted, the radiant face, the offered cup. He would have kissed the hands where the nails had been, washed the feet where the spikes had entered. Then the Lord would have sat and talked to him.

In his anguish, the cobbler cried out,

"Why is it, Lord, that your feet delay?

Have you forgotten that this was the day?"

Then, soft in the silence a voice he heard:

"Lift up your heart for I kept my word.
Three times I came to your friendly door;
Three times my shadow was on your floor.
I was the man with the bruised feet;
I was the woman you gave to eat;
I was the child on the homeless street."

LETTER 15

"When the winter of my life threatens
me with pain and death,
Leave me not in loneliness to its
cold and icy breath;
Breathe upon me from above and
enfold me in your love."

Brother Ramon SSF (1936-2000)
An Anglican Franciscan Monk
(emphasis added)

Another Day – Who is in Charge?

How long...

Dear daughter,

In this letter I will pick up where I left off and write about how life continued in the nursing home in the new year.

There were several extremely difficult months with many health and management concerns. During this time your father and I felt increasingly isolated from friends, relatives and the outside world. But that is the nature of living in a home; it can cause a sense of separation from the outside world. Perhaps friends keep away because they do not like to see the suffering that's going on, or because they don't know what to say to offer comfort, or in our case it could simply have been because it was the winter. Whatever the reason, there was a sense of being forgotten, which was not nice. Despite this, however, I knew in my heart of hearts that our friends, even if we did not see them, were standing with us in prayer, praying for us. This thought was a wonderful comfort throughout this period and I felt very thankful!

As his wife, I was particularly sensitive as to what your dad must have be going through. He had always been a very private, proud, able and clever "Englishman", who didn't need to depend on anyone. Now, sadly, he realised that his independent lifestyle was gradually being taken from him. It was so difficult for him to accept that he was losing his independence and that he needed to wait for others to do things for him – and it only seemed to get worse as his condition progressed. This change from being independent to depending on others could well be compared to clouds appearing in the sky followed by day after day of rain – the rain taking away what had once been sunny, warm and comfortable with a clear sky. This kind of dull, stormy atmosphere seemed to have the power to take away his language of hope, i.e. his sense of humour.

At that time, words of a certain poem drifted through my mind, which well expressed the kind of battle we were facing. It was the battle of the long season of winter with all its darkness hindering us from believing in the arrival of spring. I recorded this poem in my diary because I was moved by it and the words sounded like they could have come from your dad's lips.

A Better Resurrection

I have no wit, no words, no tears;
My heart within me like a stone
Is numbed too much for hopes and fears.
Look right, look left, I dwell alone;

I lift mine eyes, but dimmed with grief
No everlasting hills I see;
My life is in the falling leaf.
O Jesus, quicken me.

My life is like a faded leaf,
My harvest dwindled to a husk:
Truly my life is void and brief
And tedious in the barren dusk.

My life is like a frozen thing,
No bud nor greenness can I see,
Yet rise it shall – the sap in spring,
O Jesus, rise in me.

These verses were written by Christina Rossetti, an English poet (1830-1894) who wrote a variety of romantic, devotional and children's poems during her lifetime. She is best known for her long poem *Goblin Market*, her love poem *Remember*, and for the words of the Christmas carol *In the Bleak Midwinter*. I read that at some point in her life, she suffered a nervous breakdown and experienced bouts of depression. In the light of these, it is interesting to note what kind of words she used to describe her own life: "wilted", "barren", "meaningless and perishable", "a mere husk compared to a full harvest". From her deep anguish, see how she reaches out in hope: "O Jesus, quicken me," and, "O Jesus, rise in me, like sap does in the spring."

It was difficult to cling to what we could not see in the midst of our ongoing isolation. Your dad suffered with an extremely itchy skin, which made matters worse still. What do you do when you have an itch? You scratch – and he was no exception to this rule. His arms turned very sore and on his back and tummy he had several irritated and swollen areas; not a nice sight to look at, let alone be suffering with. Each time I arrived to visit, the carers critically reported that he was not leaving his wounds alone. By telling me this, they were hoping that I would influence him not to scratch. And so I raised the topic and tried to persuade him to leave his dressings alone. But he felt that I was taking the nurses' side, which had a negative impact on his emotions. That in turn increased his sense of isolation and lack of hope.

These daily issues seemed never-ending and felt very intense at the time. I so longed to see him free from all the suffering he was experiencing and for the relationship between him and the nursing staff to be improved. He often sighed deeply in misery, and I felt unable to bear it all whilst at the same time deeply wanting to support him.

Obviously, what I thought I could bear and what God thought I could bear differed. Left to my own choice, I would probably have decided I couldn't take any more and that I had reached my limit. But what are *my* limits and what are *God's* limits? He graciously led me to Psalm 13 in one of my conversations with him. Reading it, I realised how the psalmist longed for God to come and intervene in his 'fed up' situation, and I took comfort in the fact that here was someone else who felt what I felt. The psalmist expressed plainly to God his problem. As a result, God diverted him away from his questions and led him to consider who God is and had been in his past.

I think we all have the tendency to allow difficult circumstances to take over and drag us into believing that we can do nothing about it. Negative attitudes creep in with thoughts like, "I can't take any more," beckoning God to answer questions laid out as in the psalm:

> *How long, O LORD? Will you forget me for ever?*
> *How long will you hide your face from me?*
> *How long must I wrestle with my thoughts*
> *and every day have sorrow in my heart?*
> *How long will my enemy triumph over me?*

Look on me and answer, O LORD my God.
Give light to my eyes, or I will sleep in death;
my enemy will say, "I have overcome him,"
and my foes will rejoice when I fall...

Psalm 13:1-4

My questions were similar:

- How long, O Lord? How long must we go on?
- Where are you?
- Why are we so alone?
- Why must I wrestle with my thoughts and every day have sorrow in my heart?
- Lord, we can't see our way out; give light to our eyes, we pray.

These words did not only match our circumstances, but a similar plea was made in the poem I mentioned earlier, *A Better Resurrection* by Christina Rossetti. Both the poet and the psalmist found themselves in 'downcast circumstances' but after expressing it, saw an open window through which they received glimpses of reassurance that they were not alone in their distress. The God of hope, love and compassion was there with them. The psalmist concludes his heart-cry with the following amazing words:

But I trust in your unfailing love;
my heart rejoices in your salvation.
I will sing to the LORD,
for he has been good to me.

Psalm 13:5,6

He realised in his heart and declared with his lips that "[God] has been good to me." As a result of this focus, he shone with cheerfulness, confidence and reassurance based on what God had provided for him even in his 'hard-hitting' time. This reminded me of a verse in Isaiah 45:3a where it speaks of God having "treasures of darkness, riches stored in secret places" and the reasons that God is storing up things is to prepare us for when hard times hit us. The same verse goes on: "...so that you may know that I am the LORD ..." God's actions reveal his power and control, which leads me to believe, alongside the psalmist and the poet, that the Lord our God is beside us in all situations of life. There are treasures to be found in suffering.

From all this I took up the challenge to write my own psalm portraying my feelings of doubt, disappointment, being forgotten – but in it prove God's sufficiency for all my needs.

In Times Like These

At times I feel forgotten by you, Lord.
Helplessly stirred with fear of what is to come
with the life that's weak and forlorn,
waiting like a bulb in frosty ground
for a warmer day to come.
And so, I ask my God at such a time:
"Do you care?" "Do you know?"
"Do you see what I am seeing?"
"Do you hear and respond to my crying?"
Waiting longingly for a new day without trying.

Oh God, your words at times seem harsh,
they call to persevere and not give up:
Be faithful, trust me, do not fear, believe... and
do not stand in your own self will.

Yet, at other intervals, and truly, just at the right time,
you gently touch and affirm that
you know, understand and care,
you actually desire to be present in my doubting day.

This truth proves good enough and so
I pick it up, apply it to the scene,
and the clouds of oppression flee.
My husband still the same, circumstances have not shifted
but it is God's strength that sees me through the day.
The clock ticks symbolising 'life moves on',
sustained by 'flowing oil' on aches and pains,
thus transforming, using every inch of life's soil,

creating hope where despair breaks down,
imparting courage for the brand-new day.

Conclusion is, that it would be foolish to state, "There is no
God,"
who does not hear, see or care.
"God is, God was and always will be."
He is the great I AM, who came to earth to give his life.
My darkness is the very spot for his disclosure
of light to dawn on circumstance forlorn.
So, come what may, I choose to trust, obey
at every stage in every way, affirm without delay,
but wait and rest in God each day.

As a keen gardener, I know full well that without darkness nothing comes to birth. Without light, nothing flowers, and this means to me that life and death have to co-exist in our lives in order to bring the best in every season.

And now, my dear daughter, let me move on and recall here the amazing and unexpected surprise when we heard from you that you were on your way to visit us for two days. It was like sunshine flying from Switzerland to England to cheer us and encourage us in our ongoing trials. What a moment of hope and joy – a good reason to thank the Lord for answering prayers in a very practical and meaningful way!

You arrived on a Friday evening, we spent Saturday with your dad and you flew back on Sunday. You brought Evan, our delightful second grandchild with you, who at the time was about eight months old. This was the first time he saw his grandad, which in a way was a reminder that *life goes on.* Your coming was well timed; your presence and your visual support spoke volumes of love into our struggles. We so enjoyed Sunday lunch together in the visitors' room, it brought me great satisfaction to see your dad appreciating it, especially as the previous day he had ignored us all. Your departure soon followed, and we all felt thankful for the sparkling opportunity of having been together! Would you ever see your dad alive again, was a real question you and I posed together. Little did we know at the time that he had only some months more on this earth. However, I trust your visit was helpful in giving you fresh insight into the complexity of his care.

You saw the struggle he had with the communication, as some of the nursing staff spoke very little English. There were numerous occasions on which he anxiously complained that he did not understand what some of the carers were saying, and equally they did not understand him. At other times, he felt he was being talked *at*, rather than talked *with*, but I know that these aspects of lack in his case were not intentional – the shortage of nurses at the time was huge. While these were difficult and complicated problems that confronted us, your turning up was true evidence of God's goodness revealed through you.

Hence, I declare, *God is good and faithful, all the time!* My lesson here is that I learned that God is waiting for each of us to look for his light in dark places or, to put it another way, to remember that spring follows every winter according to the order of creation.

This brings me back to Christina Rossetti's words: "Yet rise it shall – the sap in spring, O Jesus, rise in me."

I have included in my tailpiece thoughts from my diary building on the themes in this letter but for now I wish to close with these words:

> *When we depend upon man,*
> *we get what men can do.*
> *When we depend upon prayer,*
> *we get what God can do.*

Author unknown

I greet you with a peaceful
and thankful heart

Mum

Reflection

Jesus has not promised us an easy life but he has promised that he will not leave us alone with our burdens. Rather he will sustain us and see us through day by day. I hear Jesus' own words inviting me:

> *"Come to me, all you who are weary and burdened, and I will give you rest."*

Matthew 11:28

...and he also encourages us to live one day at a time, no more and no less:

> *"Therefore, do not worry about tomorrow, for tomorrow will worry about itself. Each day has enough trouble of its own."*

Matthew 6:34

I also love the following words of Jesus:

> *"Peace I leave with you; my peace I give you. I do not give to you as the world gives. Do not let your hearts be troubled and do not be afraid."*

John 14:27

> *"I have told you these things, so that in me you may have peace. In this world you will have trouble. But take heart! I have overcome the world."*

John 16:33,34

True, he has not always changed situations as I might well have prayed, but he definitely has been willing to share pain and sorrow and thereby strengthened my call to persevere, come what may.

The following verses come from a Methodist Church magazine. They use the metaphor of a 'traffic light' to express spiritual truth. I include it here with permission of the author who prefers to remain anonymous:

The Lord of the Traffic Lights

I had to stop because the light was red
although I wanted to race ahead.
The Lord said that it was time to be still
Time to reflect and discern his will.

And there in the stillness by God's good grace
sweet communion with him had taken place
and his new purpose he began to show
and he pointed out the way I should go.

The bright amber light then began to shine
as I prepared for this journey of mine.
For the Lord my God had now equipped me
to take a different type of journey.

I had to detour and change direction
shown to me in time of reflection.
For Jesus had promised always to be
a close Companion and Guide to me.

Then as I waited the light turned green
and I set off through a different scene.
From the old I travelled into the new
as the Lord was showing me what to do.

Sometimes the light turned green, amber or red.
Sometimes I stopped, prepared for what's ahead.
But at all times God was in full control
of the traffic lights directing my soul.

LETTER 16

"Trust in the Lord with all
your heart and lean not
on your own understanding;
in all your ways acknowledge him,
and he will make your paths straight.
Do not be wise in your own eyes;
fear the Lord and shun evil."

Proverbs 3:5-7

Flies on Wounds – Bearing the Pain

Even horses...

Dearest Helen,

What do you think of my title for this letter? A little unusual, you might well say whilst at the same time wondering what it is all about. Let me explain!

Our women's group at church used to organise an annual weekend away lasting from Friday afternoon to Sunday afternoon. After careful thought, I prepared myself to join a fairly large number of women for the event. But as the day of departure approached, I started to get nervous about it. I realised how very tired I was and the very thought of having to face a crowd of happy people felt overwhelming. I also had in mind that your dad was increasingly struggling, his health completely breaking down, and nothing seemed to cheer him. With everything looking so miserable, I found myself reconsidering whether to go or not. I found myself repeatedly saying things like, "It is best that I should stay with him. He needs me." In other words, a part of me felt it would be better to stay with him rather than to have time for myself.

Decision, decision – but the 'weekend away' won!

Looking back on it now, I am so thankful that I had the courage to join the others, because the change of scenery was invaluable in giving me time to think, to listen, to share and to cry, as well as to have a good meal and be alone in listening to God.

Glenfall House is a retreat centre in Cheltenham, Gloucester, set in beautiful countryside, surrounded by a huge garden and spacious rooms. I truly could not have asked for a better location. The welcome and evening meal were a real treat, and after that we had our first session by the weekend speaker. The theme was all about how the devil tries to deceive us into keeping away from what God wants for us. I felt that what I heard was 'spot on' with regard to what was going on in our circumstances. I had almost not gone on the break due to my indecisiveness, but once I was there I realised that it was going to be a

God-appointed time. God was going to work in and through me in this place, showing me his counsel and what he had in mind for me.

The following is just the tiniest part of what I'd like to share with you from this trip. Along with what I heard taught, there were questions whirling in my heart and mind for which no answers were immediately forthcoming. For some time, I pondered over this topic of how the devil tries to trick us into believing something that is not true.

Eventually, I remembered a specific scripture that I believed directly applied to what was being taught at the event. The verse can be found in John 10:10.

> *"The thief [the devil] comes only to steal and kill and destroy; but I [Jesus] have come that they [mankind] may have life and have it to the full."*

I felt incredibly blessed as I discovered for myself that the devil is always seeking to take away what God provides so freely. Strangely, I had always known of the devil's plan – to kill, to destroy and to steal – but this time it touched an inner sensitive cord of mine because it felt personal. It was a complete eye-opener, a word that was meant for me, teaching me how to distinguish between God's purpose in all walks of life (such us to build up, protect, teach valuable lessons, and provide a full and meaningful life) and what makes Satan happy (stealing, killing and destroying life).

This contrast showed how amazingly wonderful the power and relevance of the word of God are; at the right time and in the right place, it acted like medicine for my sick soul. From that moment, I distinctly knew that my weekend was not going to be wasted but that its purpose would be nourishment for my ongoing journey.

At times I found it so very easy to be busy with life and its problems and consequently push God out, while it would be far better to focus my attention on him. Now and then, over my life, I have neglected to go to God first, but nevertheless realise afresh that it is truly important to stand aside from the cares of life by taking regular time out for a specific purpose such as to pray, listen, rest and read the word of God, specifically to realign my self-centredness to his will. In this way my story continues just like the night passes with the dawning of a new day.

The next day I went on a morning stroll, and as I walked through some of the local countryside, I learned more of what God had in store for me. I noticed beautiful horses grazing in the field. They fed themselves contentedly as they moved along the grass. Their eyes were blinkered with shields and a blanket protected their backs from various pests. My eyes were drawn to a horse swishing his tail from side to side looking restless in these peaceful surroundings. I wondered why it did this. And then my searching eyes noticed swarms of flies on an area of its unprotected skin; *no wonder!* The other horses were not disturbed in the same way, as their cover was more comprehensively laid over their body. *Interesting,* I thought, as I watched this poor animal who clearly was in trouble with flies on its back, irritating it so much that it could do nothing else but swish its tail from side to side to keep the flies, its enemy, at bay.

In this moment, I suddenly remembered having similar flies, a similar enemy, trying to irritate and settle on the bare skin of our 'circumstances'. I couldn't help listening to the voice within telling me that I too could use the 'tail of Jesus', meaning the *name* of Jesus, to flick off the flies that had the only intention to settle and cause harm to the raw circumstances of our lives. Throughout the day, I was deeply aware that God wanted me to use the 'tail of Jesus' by experiencing a spirit of praise instead of a spirit of despair, and his Spirit went on to speak to me a few more encouragements, such as forgiveness and love being bound together and having the capacity to bring peace and victory to our existing circumstances.

The entire retreat weekend turned out to be like a strong and colourful rope coming down from heaven to 'my earth' calling me to hold on tight and be rescued from the devil's devices in what lay ahead!

As you might well imagine, life had not changed at the nursing home in my absence. The same carers were still organising each day and looking after your dad, who remained in great need. But the beauty was that I felt *I* had changed, refreshed by the word of God and by supporting people, causing me to stand, as it were, on a spacious place of courage and with a determination to rely on God's strength. I felt assured, once again, that his ways are perfect, his word is flawless, he is a shield to all who take refuge in him and he will keep my lamp burning with hope to the end.

I want to tell you now about another heavenly surprise that fell into my apron, and on reflection it linked so amazingly with the above.

An unexpected CD arrived with the post. It contained teaching from someone in Switzerland and I soon found that the message being taught was knocking at the door of my heart. Let me describe in a few words the impact this teaching had on me after having taken time to listen to the CD, beginning with a verse from the letter to the Romans:

And we know that in all things God works for the good of those who love him, who have been called according to his purpose.

Romans 8:28

This is a passage that I knew by heart and often quoted to myself and others. I was filled with astonishment at *how exactly right* these words were as the emphasis was on *all* things, which meant nothing was to be left out that is happening in our lives. God, if we let him, will use each opportunity to bring good out of every situation. This is good news and very significant, especially when the outlook looks bleak.

Then, I was flabbergasted when I heard the pastor talk about flies; yes, *flies!* He said something like this: "Flies are attracted to wounds and prevent the wounds from healing. We all have wounds – wounds that come with life – and many people carry their wounds all their lives, allowing flies to settle on them and harm them in the most unexpected ways."

The mention of flies settling and harming made me think about the experience God had given me in the field with the horses. So I had no problem linking this message with the picture and lesson I had been given there.

All this strengthened the warning I had been given: of not letting the enemy have the upper hand in experiences of life – oh, so timely, special and affirming!

As I am reflecting back on some of my struggles, I do realise afresh that in all situations I had been given a choice of either focusing on the problem and ploughing on with it, or taking time to listen and use each opportunity to trust God and follow his counsel.

I also suspect that sometimes we have to reach rock bottom before God lifts us up. Logically speaking, how else could we testify to having been rescued or strengthened, or even given understanding, unless we have experienced failure and downfall? God is gracious, and so I consider it a blessing to seek his voice on everything that comes into my life.

I feel it is important that I share these experiences with you, in order to give you a better understanding of who I am, how I manage the affairs of life and how I persevere and nurture my belief in an all-knowing God; he is sovereign in all his ways and his love has no limits.

Let me close this letter with Psalm 143:8-10. I love to use the words as my own prayer:

> *Let the morning bring me word*
> *of your unfailing love,*
> *for I have put my trust in you.*
> *Show me the way I should go,*
> *for to you I lift up my soul.*
> *Rescue me from my enemies, O LORD,*
> *for I hide myself in You.*
> *Teach me to do your will,*
> *for you are my God;*
> *may your good Spirit lead me on level ground.*

Amen! I thank you for reading my continuous story.

I love you,

Your Mum

Reflection

I love the character of Peter in the Bible. One moment he is full of enthusiasm but then a few minutes later is filled with doubt and fear. In Matthew 14, Peter is called by Jesus to walk towards him on the water. He dares to step out of his boat, placing his feet firmly on the water, and he does the impossible. However, he nearly sinks when he focuses on the howling wind. And why does this happen? We read:

> *Then Peter got out of the boat, walked on the water and came toward Jesus. But when Peter saw the wind, he became afraid and beginning to sink, cried out, "Lord, save me!"*
>
> *Matthew 14:29,30*

As Peter saw the wind, he became insecure and afraid and lost sight of what Jesus had enabled him to do. But Peter knew what to do in this alarming situation. He cried out to Jesus for help and he was saved from drowning.

Are we not the same? One moment I have enough faith to believe that Jesus is all I need but at other times allow myself to be drowned by fear because the winds of life blow so intensely. The good news is that Jesus only wants me/us to ask for his help.

I love looking up the meaning of words and so I looked up the word 'sovereign' in the dictionary and found words and phrases like 'superior', 'greatest', 'supreme in power', 'ruler'. These words simply emphasise that God has no limits. Therefore, I delight to be a witness to the evidence of God's immeasurable goodness in every moment of my life.

I was so struck today at how amazingly we can be inspired by different Bible translations. The words can speak out to us refreshingly in modern and traditional translations alike. The words below are just what I needed to hear. It is the Lord and his words that will keep me on track rather than looking at the raging sea and storm around me. God is faithful!

> *Trust God from the bottom of your heart; don't try to figure out everything on your own. Listen for God's voice in*

everything you do, everywhere you go; he's the one who will keep you on track. Don't assume you know it all. Run to God! Run from evil!

Proverbs 3:5-7 (MSG)

Trust in the LORD with all your heart
　and lean not on your own understanding;
in all your ways acknowledge him,
　and he will make your path straight.
Do not be wise in your own eyes;
　fear the LORD and shun evil.

Proverbs 3:5-7

LETTER 17

"Have mercy on me,
O God, have mercy on me,
for in you my soul takes refuge.
I will take refuge in the shadow of your wings
until the disaster has passed. ...
Be exalted, O God, above the heavens;
let your glory be over all the earth."

Psalm 57:1,5

Another Example – Job and His Suffering

Encounters through friends...

Hello Helen,

This letter describes another God-encounter appearing out of the blue into my life. I feel that these special incidences are like gifts from God to be received and unwrapped, to be used and shared with others. So I decided to share this one with you.

One day, friends from London visited us at the nursing home and at the end of their visit the wife took me aside, looked at me in earnest and said, "What your husband is going through reminds me of Job, who suffered similarly with sores from head to toe."

The interesting aspect at the time was that our friends who mentioned this had no idea that I was already carrying the story of Job in my heart. I was aiming to learn from his example how to stay focused on God in what I saw as our 'season of suffering'. So the connection our friends made was not at all surprising. I rather took it as a confirmation from God, reminding me that he was involved. He was giving me more insight into what was to come.

Let me elaborate on these sudden pauses that seem to occur in life's circumstances and the way we may respond to them. At times, it seems that these appear as unimportant, and we enforce this feeling by raising our eyebrows muttering something like, "Oh, yes," aiming to avoid the issue for whatever reason while moving on to something totally different. For example, in my case, I would have denied what was going on in my true inner self – but I chose to *listen*. So instead of avoidance, I accepted the truth of my friend's comment.

Returning to the story of Job, the author of the book is unknown although some critics say that it was possibly Job himself who wrote it. Personally, I take the fact that as it is recorded in the Bible as showing that its message bears importance for everyone. The story describes in great detail how a loving God allowed horrendous suffering on this man's life – which makes it an uncomfortable read. But because of my friend's reference, I continued reading and meditating on it. I wrote some of my personal thoughts down – what I gleaned from the story and how it applied to my circumstances. So I am including some of my findings and am repeatedly startled at how applicable the word of God remains, even though it was written thousands of years ago.

The telling of Job's story could easily be compared to watching a film on a stage with picture after picture showing one scene of suffering after another. It grips the viewers with bewilderment that such a faithful servant of God had to endure such anguish. Furthermore, the Bible tells us that in a very short space of time Job lost everything: his wealth (he had great material goods), all of his children (seven sons and three daughters) and his health (afflicted with painful sores from the soles of his feet to the top of his head). Even his wife said:

> *"Are you still holding on to your integrity? Curse God and die!"*
>
> *Job 2:9*

But do you know what Job's response was to his wife who showed no interest in his suffering? He honoured God as he replied:

> *"You are talking like a foolish woman. Shall we accept good from God, and not trouble?"*
>
> *Job 2:10*

Job continued honouring God and he never rejected or blamed God for anything that was happening to him. Rather, when devastating news reached him, he grieved deeply but continued worshipping and trusting God. Yes, in the midst of it all we are informed that he struggled with his faith. He inundated God and his friends with question after question. He argued and complained that he was being treated unfairly. Yet, in all his endless tragedies he did not deviate from trusting the faithful and true God. What a truly inspiring example!

It has become my own personal goal that also, like Job, I might never lose sight of the Almighty God. However, this is easier said than done; as we both know, when going through any crisis, the tendency is to blame God, to question him and even expect explanations as to why certain tragedies have become part of our lives. We exclaim, "Why me? What have I done? Why these unending troubling circumstances?" We might even moan over what we don't have rather than what we do have. But Job's story gives me new energy to aim high and to choose not to lose sight of God's faithfulness. Do I need answers to my why's? Yes, it would be convenient to have answers to the why's of life; but I have come to believe that God has already provided enough information about himself. After all, has he not created me? Does he not hold all things together? Is he not the Lord over heaven and earth? And the One who gave up his Son, Jesus, for me and indeed for mankind? Oh, there is so much more to God and his existence than I can express.

Like Job, I have plenty of evidence and reasons to trust him. I do want to say it again: I truly believe that "in all things God works for the good of those who love him, who have been called according to his purpose".

And so at this point I bow my head in devotion to God and pray, "Lord, my God, I do realise that my small view of you can block the way for you to draw closer. I repent from saying wrong words and having wrong attitudes, especially in unexpected circumstances that are difficult, painful and inexplicable. Please, I pray, take control with all your fullness in all areas of my life. Help me, Lord, by your indwelling Holy Spirit, to follow your truth and let it reign in and over me. May I, in all things, patiently wait for the outcome, seeking your greatness, generosity and infinite love to direct my thoughts and words, through Jesus Christ my Saviour and Lord. Amen!"

A local friend sent me the following words of a hymn that meant a lot to me at the time. It speaks so courageously about 'being still' and trusting God's steadfastness despite the roughness of the sea of life.

Still, my soul, be still, and do not fear,
though winds of change may rage tomorrow.
God is at your side; no longer dread
the fires of unexpected sorrow.

Still, my soul, be still, do not be moved
by lesser lights and fleeting shadows.
Hold on to his ways with shield of faith
against temptation's flaming arrows.

Still, my soul, be still, do not forsake
the Truth you learned in the beginning.
Wait upon the Lord and hope will rise
as stars appear when day is dawning.

Chorus:
God, you are my God, and I will trust
In you and not be shaken.
Lord of peace, renew a steadfast spirit
within me ... to rest in you alone. [21]

Stuart Townend

God be praised; for knows what he is doing! I accept that the struggles will go on, but his shining light brings understanding and purpose to the unknown. For this I am thankful; I am helped to press on with life as it presents itself.

I trust that you are blessed as you share in the surprises of my life.

Your Mum

---

[21] Extract taken from the song 'Still My Soul' by S. Townend. Copyright © Thankyou Music*

Reflection

"Do not ask what circumstances will do to you today; ask, rather, what you will do with your circumstances through prayer." I like this!

I recorded in my diary a time when your dad rang me – he had had a troubled night scenario. As he told his story, I felt helplessly lost for words, sad and empty. At the same time, my eyes faced the window and I saw the sun was shining on this new day. In that moment I received peace as I was reminded of God's faithfulness however troubled the morning felt. Indeed, this gave me a good reason for being thankful even though I was not in the mood.

Prayer: "Thank you, Lord, for reminding me of the words of truth found in the Bible that I have set to memory: 'The steadfast love of the LORD never ceases; his mercies never come to an end; they are new every morning; great is your faithfulness.'"

Helpful quotes as I pondered on the above situation:

Life is like a rainbow. You need both the sun and the rain to make its colours appear.

Author unknown

Difficult roads often lead to beautiful destinations.

Author unknown

Consider what God has done: Who can straighten what he has made crooked? When times are good, be happy; but when times are bad, consider: God has made the one as well as the other. Therefore, a man cannot discover anything about his future.

Ecclesiastes 7:13,14

An anonymous entry in my diary called 'From a forgotten friend':

How are you? Just had to send a note to tell you how much I love you and care about you.

I saw you yesterday and you were walking with your friends. I waited all day hoping you would want to talk to me as well. As evening drew near, I gave you a sunset to close your day, and a cool breeze to rest you, and I waited. You never came. Yes, it did hurt me, but I still love you because I am your friend.

I saw you fall asleep last night and longed to touch your brow, so I spilled moonlight on your pillow and your face. Again, I waited, wanting to rush down so we could talk. I have so many gifts for you. You awakened late this morning and rushed off to work; my tears were in the rain.

Today you looked so sad, so all alone. It makes my heart ache, because I understand, my friends let me down too and hurt me so many times... but I love you! I try to tell you in the blue sky and in the quiet green grass. I whisper in the leaves on the trees and breathe in the colours of the flowers. I shout to you in the mountain streams and give the birds a love song. I clothe you with warm sunshine and perfume the air with nature's scents.

My love for you is deeper than the oceans, and bigger than the biggest want or need in your heart. Oh, if only you knew how much I want to help you. I want you to meet my Father and he wants to help you too. Just call me and ask for me.

Talk with me. But please, please don't forget me. I have so much to tell you.

Prayer: "Father God, in the name of Jesus, help me to saturate my thinking with your thoughts, with your words and your love so that my thoughts may be more and more taken up with eternal realities rather than the world's values. Thank you! Amen!"

LETTER 18

"God is the only absolute reality.
All else is relative.
If we wish to live in the light
of God's presence,
we need to discern the real
and the unreal.
Choosing what is real
increases the light.
The unreal holds us in the dark."

Kathleen O'Sullivan SSL (1935-2019)
Light Out of Darkness[22]

---

[22] Hodder & Stoughton (1993)

No Turning Back – Journeying

A new song...

My beautiful Helen,

I have always been a person who lingers and seeks to explore the reality of life, and the following phrase summarises my view when coming to a conclusion:

If we wish to live in the light of God's presence, we need to discern the real from the unreal. Only God is the absolute reality. All else is relative.

Kathleen O'Sullivan

Additionally, as I discern realities, they act like a wakeup call. My comfortable make-believe world is stirred, and I find myself feeling that life has come to a real and uncomfortable standstill. I thankfully realise that this painful truth is not to be feared since God is in charge of all that is real. My reflection on the unknown 'field of life', I believe, has a tendency for creating fear and may therefore hinder me from trusting God for what lies ahead. Fear is a scary and dark emotion that excludes the light from shining. But God is light, and his desire is to dispel darkness; to shine and to illuminate, bringing hope and clarity.

Let me share with you another one of these wakeup calls that I received from God through a phone call. The voice on the phone shocked me: "Tell your husband to let go of what he has because something far better is waiting for him – eternal life. Believe that this future life is far superior than lying in bed, sitting all day in a wheelchair, forcing down meals and generally struggling with daily existence."

At first, I took offence at the directness of the caller's words. *How could anyone be so upfront?* I said to myself. At that moment I experienced a 'standstill' followed by a recognition of the stark reality of our situation: we simply could not accept the poor quality of your dad's life and face the reality of the inevitable forthcoming separation.

His death was bound to come. It was truly strange how many times I had been 'wishing' in my heart an arrival of the end but had always avoided facing the subject for different reasons. Today, reality had arrived, and could be neither hidden nor feared. I was to obey and share this with your dad.

I was amazed how well he responded to this sombre and difficult communication. After all, his family was the only thing left to cling on to in his otherwise empty existence of suffering. Remarkably, he recognised and verbalised his need to release you, his daughter, and his grandchildren, to live their lives without him. He expressed that he must stop clutching on to his sisters who were both older than him. He loved them dearly. He was remarkably open speaking about these issues, which to me was a confirmation that the message was based in reality and meant for our future good.

A Bible verse spontaneously sprung to mind confirming that our God was skilfully handling our situation:

What, then, shall we say in response to these things? If God is for us, who can be against us?

Romans 8:31

I reflect on the life of our past four years, confessing that my survival kit had held many unrealistic wishes. One of the wishes turning up from time to time was literally to be free from the circumstances that bound me so heavily to the place of the nursing home in which he and I had to live. At those times, I felt I had lost my life, and selfishly longed to have it back again on my terms. Not to be in control or in charge of circumstances was such a difficult lesson to learn. The issue had a habit of turning up again and again. My dictionary defines 'Let go of' as 'relinquish one's grip on someone or something'. And so on that day, after the phone call, the 'let go' meant something that was real to us both, but in different ways. Your dad dealt with it well and I too had to let go in earnest in allowing him to die; to let him go to the place of his eternal future which I trusted would be far better than his life here on earth. Of course, I only knew after this event that the timing had been exactly right; none of us knew when my friend's message came that he had only a little time left here on earth.

This, then, is how it happened.

Dramatic changes took place when a call at 7am on Sunday morning, 10th June 2007, informed me that the man who had suffered so much had come to the end of his earthly life. Immediately, I got dressed and made my way to the nursing home and entered his room.

I was surprised at how well he looked, his arms folded on his chest, which reminded me of his rugby-playing times. His face was absolutely peaceful and his facial skin shining. I stayed with him for two solid hours.

The atmosphere in his room was tangibly serene. From a CD the Welsh Male Voice Choir sang hymns that we both had become accustomed to listening to over the past few weeks. I reflected how we had both loved the songs and often sang along when we knew the words; even the carers had tended to put the CD on when they cared for him. It was magnificent to hear the rich harmonious voices singing, for example, *How Great Thou Art* and *The Old Rugged Cross*. It truly filled his room with peace and a concrete sense of wellbeing, confirming yet again that God's sovereignty is over life and death. For me the following Bible text expresses his loving authority so clearly:

> *For my thoughts are not your thoughts, neither are your ways my ways, declares the LORD. As the heavens are higher than the earth, so are my ways higher than your ways and my thoughts than your thoughts. As the rain and the snow come down from heaven, and do not return to it without watering the earth and making it bud and flourish, so that it yields seed for the sower and bread for the eater, so is my word that goes out from my mouth: It will not return to me empty, but accomplish what I desire and achieve the purpose for which I sent it. You will go out in joy and be led forth in peace, the mountains and the hills will burst into songs before you, and all the trees of the field will clap their hands. Instead of the thorn bush will grow the pine tree, and instead of briers the myrtle will grow. This will be for the LORD's renown, for an everlasting sign, which will not be destroyed.*
>
> Isaiah 55:8-13

So now, on this Sunday morning, I sat there! Different carers knocked on the door as they turned up for duty, giving me a hug of sympathy. Many of them had tears flowing even though he had had many disagreements with them and at times had spoken with harshness. Somehow it had made him the person that they loved and appreciated.

The night sister said, "You have completed your promise," to which I asked, "What do you mean?" She simply answered, "Until death do us part." These words were more meaningful to me than this particular sister could have realised, as I had often felt limited and inadequate in my relationship with him. I believe that I needed to hear these words there and then for my own comfort in the days ahead.

As I looked back over his life, I recalled how very able, conscientious and loyal he was; how he looked after everything in our house and home, took charge of the finance and loved being at home more than anywhere else in the whole world. He was always willing to keep the decor of the interior of our home in good condition, and never missed putting a nail in the right place and at the right time. All his handiwork was delivered to perfection.

He simply loved being busy around his home – but unfortunately all these pleasures came to an end through his ill health, which had lasted many years. Circumstances developed beyond his control, yet he learned to accept them and live with them on a daily basis. To depend on others was no easy task. In fact, I feel really proud of him as I realise how willing he was to accept what he could not change. True, for many reasons his life became difficult and frustrating, but we both knuckled down to live it as it presented itself. In his room we shared many hours sitting together because there was no other place we could go, and with this our relationship was enhanced more than words can ever express or explain. Even the negative aspects of this time empowered us to be together in a positive and meaningful way. For me as his wife, it was such a privilege to be involved with his ups and downs and to show him repeatedly that I cared for and loved him just as he was. My one and only desire at the time was to live in faithful commitment to him. To help me in this I made a few of my own rules which I repeatedly had to learn to apply:

- to be utterly loyal, focused and committed to the situation we could not change;
- to simply sit with Jesus and talk to him about my daily struggles;
- to persevere in remaining positive;
- to be thankful in all things.

My love and commitment were grounded by having 'time out' with God, which gradually became my source of strength, motivating me with purpose in good and bad times. It is incredible how the word of God always came to my spirit with meaning, touching places where I was hurting, crying, despairing, confused or just did not know how to proceed. At other times I was encouraged and strengthened through what I saw in nature or through friendships. At night, when I could find no rest, I lit a night candle reminding myself that Jesus gives, and is, light, and so in the company of this symbolism I was able to rest and sleep.

Looking back, I am filled with worship to God, praising him as the source of life and death, of all things in heaven and on earth. All is under his control. And in my experience, he is the One who provides a way in the desert, offers water when thirsty and leads with certainty to new things. He brings comfort in believing that the remainder of my time here on earth is in his hands.

As I was lost in thought with open and empty hands, which were being filled with treasured things of the past, this moment was broken by the door being slowly opened by the undertaker. This marked that the long years of my sitting in this room had come to the end.

After the above events, the funeral followed on 19th June 2007 – and what a day it was! It was so wonderful to have you, my daughter, and your husband and the grandchildren here. You and your children arrived on 13th June and stayed until 4th July. Your husband came for two days which I appreciated very much. Death is always sad for those left behind, but for us it also turned out to be a blessed occasion, challenging but amazing.

The service took place at Nettlebed Church, and your dad was buried in the churchyard, as this was want he had wanted. The place of worship was packed to the full with family and friends from all walks of life. Some dear friends of mine were so very helpful in planning and seeing that the service of thanksgiving went smoothly with music, pictures and food.

In the actual service, *The Grimethorpe Colliery Band* CD played *Cwm Rhondda* while his coffin was carried by six men to the front of the church. On the way out to the cemetery, *Swing Low, Sweet Chariot* took over. During the service we also watched a DVD with pictures from your dad's life, which was moving beyond words, and we were all aware of each other's tears. Although the whole service was memorable, these were some of the poignant moments.

Three of our friends and the manager of the nursing home gave a wonderful tribute to Des's life and none could help but comment on his humour. Someone even selected some of his jokes that he used repeatedly in the nursing home room, in order to divert his visitors from his own situation. Let me remind you of one or two:

> *Q: What lies at the bottom of the ocean and shakes?*
> *A: A nervous wreck!*

> *Two snakes slide into a jungle.*
> *"Are we poisonous?" asked one of the other.*
> *"I think so but why are you asking me?"*
> *"Because I just bit my tongue!"*

> *Customer to the waiter: "This roast chicken is cold."*
> *The waiter's response: "I should hope so, sir; it has been dead for about two weeks."*

And the following one he absolutely loved and recited repeatedly with his mischievous beam:

> *A man is not old when his hair turns grey,*
> *A man's not old if a tooth decays,*
> *But he's getting towards his last long sleep*
> *When his mind makes appointments his body can't keep.*

Jean, a lovely elderly church friend, courageously sang a solo in his honour, which was a special moment. Our minister and friend,

Barry Kirk, led the service sensitively and movingly. He told the congregation how Des had surrendered his life to Jesus, which happened only three weeks before he died. This is how is came about:

On 29th May 2007 your dad requested that the pastor would come to give him Holy Communion, which at the time startled me as he had never taken part in this church event before. Barry arrived within a day of this wish and with the help of his guidance, your dad asked Jesus to become a true part of his life, confessed his sins and accepted Christ Jesus as his Saviour. When asked to confess his sin, he mischievously said, "All my sin, even the ones I don't feel sorry about?" with a big smile on his face! It all turned out to be a relaxed and straightforward occasion and although he'd had many similar opportunities in his past, he had never verbalised confession and acceptance of a personal Christian faith. As I mentioned before, we had no idea at that time that this event would be one of the last conversations he would hold here on earth.

After Barry left the room, your dad asked me to tell his sister Myra what he had just done. This request demonstrated to me that he had taken the decision seriously. Jesus had become real to him there and then. A few days later he had another heavy stroke which left him semiconscious and unable to communicate, and the days that followed were very uncomfortable to watch for everyone concerned.

The effect that that story had on people present was interesting; after the service someone commented, "Who would have thought that Des would be used as an evangelist at his funeral?" Why did she make such a comment? Well, she knew Des well and was aware that he was a very private man and would not have spoken to others about his relationship with God. So I reflected that in hearing about your dad's encounter with Jesus, Des was indeed used to evangelise the hearts of people in the service.

After the service, friends from the church and my dear Malaysian friends served a wonderful tea that included sandwiches, strawberries and cream, and delicious cakes. With the sun showing its smiling face, it felt like a joyous tea party on the church lawn with people mixing well, all contributing to a genuinely happy, peaceful and amazing atmosphere.

Your dad's body was buried at a wonderful location, close to a big oak tree with a seat underneath. I believe firmly that he would have been proud of the way the service was conducted, and of how people spoke about him and how his grave was close to an oak tree. And so this important day came to an end. He has gone ahead of us to the place of 'eternal rest' and one day it will be my turn to follow.

The gravestone was laid many weeks later with the following inscription:

G.H.D. Griffiths – Des –
26.10.1928 – 10.06.2007
"My Eyes are Fixed on Jesus"

Why did I choose this phrase for his tombstone? Well, it goes back to a very significant moment when Barry arrived for the giving of the communion. He greeted Des in his wheelchair and then sat down opposite him. Before anything was said, your dad spontaneously came out with an unusual and amusing question:

"Have you come to talk to me about fixing?"

"What fixing?" asked Barry.

Your dad responded, "I remember that last time you were here you said, 'Des, keep your eyes fixed on Jesus.'"

Therefore, posing this question led the two men to talk about Jesus; why Jesus came to this earth and the meaning of the Holy Communion.

It was an amazing holy moment in our lives and this is the reason I chose the inscription.

After you had returned to Switzerland, some very difficult days and weeks followed. I felt like a lost sheep wandering around, searching for new grazing ground. My old field, the nursing home where I had spent hours over the last four years, had vanished, and with it my purpose for living. It was difficult at first to focus on using my time, as the sudden stripping of responsibilities and caring for your dad had vanished. I felt nothing could take its place. Obviously, circumstances had changed, resulting in emptiness, restlessness and depression – but thanks be to God and friends who stood by me, I accepted the challenge of learning adjustment to a new life situation.

So thank you, Lord, that by your Spirit you live in me. I belong to you and you belong to me today and forever. Jesus, you are my way, my truth and my life. Help me to walk and talk and live your way. Amen!

A big hug to you,

Mum

Reflection

I have written here some words that underpinned my continuous desire to follow what I believed:

Lord, it is truly good to be your vessel
Lord, it is great to have your life in me
It is wonderful to have seeds given and
Sow them continuously for thee.

Lord, I want to hear you clearly
When you say, let go and die
Help me to listen and be quiet
So your life may rise in mine.

Lord, you changed water into wine
You gave sight to the blind
Thirsty and hungry people you did not turn away
But totally communicated what is your way.

Lord, I thank you, for holding me important
Help me to let go and say, your will be done
Let your life within me prosper and
reach to my neighbour with your glow.

And the following psalm spoke very much to my heart with renewed hope as I stepped out into the next phase of life. God was in charge and this psalm declares it – and I was the witness of it!

Sing to the LORD a new song;
  sing to the LORD, all the earth.
Sing to the LORD, praise his name;
  proclaim his salvation day after day.
Declare his glory among the nations,
  his marvellous deeds among all peoples.
For great is the LORD and most worthy of praise;
  he is to be feared above all gods.

For all the gods of the nations are idols,
    but the LORD made the heavens.
Splendour and majesty are before him;
    strength and glory are in his sanctuary.
Ascribe to the LORD, O families of nations,
    ascribe to the LORD glory and strength.
Ascribe to the LORD the glory due his name;
    bring an offering and come into his courts.
Worship the LORD in the splendour of his holiness;
    tremble before him, all the earth.
Say among the nations, "The LORD reigns."
The world is firmly established; it cannot be moved;
    he will judge the peoples with equity.
Let the heavens rejoice, let the earth be glad;
    let the sea resound, and all that is in it;
    let the fields be jubilant, and everything in them.
Then all the trees of the forest sing for joy;
    they will sing before the LORD, for he comes,
    he comes to judge the earth.
He will judge the world in righteousness
    and the peoples in his truth.

Psalm 96

LETTER 19

"This what the past is for!
Every experience God gives us,
every person he puts in our lives
is the perfect preparation
for the future that only he can see."

Corrie ten Boom (1892-1983)
The Hiding Place (1971)

"Yes" to Life – "Yes" to Realities

In his hands...

Dear daughter,

In this letter I want to write to you about my new life as a widow. At first it was a great challenge. My previous four years had been very programmed and that had been tough. But now, I found that the newfound freedom and independence were also a struggle – how was I to handle this new situation? At times, I just longed to be living closer to you. Thoughts flitted through my mind: *How I would love to see and be near Helen's family; to see the grandchildren growing up would feel like a privilege, bliss! Who knows what my future holds? Could it be a return to my country of birth? The possibility fills me with excitement but at the same time I lack energy to dream the impossible. Lord, show me the way, I pray!*

Ironically, in my freedom I felt trapped, finding no comfort in what had passed nor in what life now held. I particularly dreaded the weekends; they were so quiet. I often did not know how to cope with my frame of mind and felt like the waves in the sea being tossed back and forth, with no definite purpose for the future. As I mentioned in a previous letter, I often tried to avoid the reality of the situations I found myself in, which sometimes led to making selfish choices. I would forget to focus on what was of value in each situation and allow myself to be pulled down, rather than learn from what I was going through.

It was not all doom and gloom though. In this current situation, I discovered afresh that to be outdoors had a positive effect on my life. I started to step outside my four walls. It majestically removed from me the sting of being alone and restored some fresh energy. It provided me with a heart that felt lighter. God's Spirit stirred me towards companionship with him again, thus helping me to look away from self to his wonderful and awesome creative work.

Here is an example:

I went to church. On my return home I started to feel isolated, deflated and simply alone. This was a common experience for me when returning from church in those days. I repeatedly felt that *they* were avoiding me; *they* had nothing to say! But on this Sunday there was a breakthrough. I made the decision not to sulk within my own safe boundaries. With a bit of effort, I ventured straight out and walked among the open fields. I felt blessed and refreshed. It was very helpful, and I kept repeating it as my need arose. *Thank you, Lord!*

"Do to others what you would have them do to you"[23] became a new motto at the time. I was learning afresh to reach out to others. I discovered voluntary work and numerous other activities which gave me a different perspective on life. I also became thankful for my daily health and strength. Hence, my life slowly gained momentum.

Of course, I also appreciate that my faith was and is in an active, loving and caring God. He is alive and he speaks, he knows me, and I in return will listen and follow his Spirit.

I am reminded here of a week's retreat I attended in Switzerland some years ago. The subjects that we contemplated were of great importance and impact. I have never forgotten the good it did and the way it strengthened my core beliefs. The theme was about God's character, about God's yes to life, no matter the circumstances of the here and now. After all, is he not the Author of all life? This, at the time, was music to my ears! As life went on, I continued to chew over the teaching from that time and, thankfully, every time I found myself understanding a little more of God's purposes for my life.

How do I learn to differentiate between unreal / illusory / false ideas and the truth that is being presented to me through the word of God? What is temporal, what is eternal? What is important while here on earth? How and when are God's promises being fulfilled?

My letters to you testify that with God's help, I have been able to pursue the 'seeds' of hope, of life, that I discovered through the word and the Spirit of God. God's word transformed and reformed my view of my life, although I had often needed to renew my yes to God. I have never been disappointed! So with a thankful heart, let me share some of what I wrote into my diary many years ago.

---

[23] Luke 6:13

God's 'yes' to me is essential for my being. The way I accept what God has offered will reflect the way I see myself and accept myself and others. Therefore, my heart's desire has been nothing less than to seek, to learn and to grow, in order to become the person God planned for me. 'Yes', because God is the Source of life, the Creator and sustains what he has created. It is his design that my life (all life) should bring him joy. This is such a wow factor for a person with a background like mine!

'Yes' to the temporal and 'yes' to the immortal / eternal way of life. The Bible text supports the theme that life here on earth is not permanent. At a glance these words could sound rather depressing, but it is the truth that "My days are like the evening shadow; I wither away like grass." (Ps. 102:11)

'Yes' to all that is passing away and 'yes' to what is eternal. Learning to live with these tensions of the material, temporal and eternal is rewarding. God's life will never finish. Everything that God allows in my life may bring me closer to him. And living closer to God gives me courage to continue looking for what is eternal in my here and now, and hold it at every cost. Each day of life becomes a gift of God.

'Yes' to God's promises in Jesus Christ ... Jesus said: "Because I live, you [I] also will live."[24] Wonderful! Yes, 'trust and believe' is something I do, no ifs or buts. If doubt creeps in, I go back to the truth which will guide me positively through my doubts. Jesus is the way, the truth and the life...

'Yes' to reality in this world and the truth of God ... this has been important. Especially, understanding the difference between reality and our own idealism, which can

---

[24] John 14:19b

overshadow the truth of a situation and appear to be true when it clearly is not.

Yes, I am willing to accept the truth as I look at life, from the outside to the inside. But I am also willing to give my yes (even though I might not feel like it) as I look at my life from the inside to the outside.

What amazing wisdom of God! He knows so much better what transformation needs to take place in order to live for his glory.

Greetings and love,

Mum

Reflection

St Francis' Prayer

Lord,
make me an instrument of your peace.
Where there is hatred, let me sow love;
where there is injury, pardon;
where there's doubt, faith;
where there is despair, hope;
where there is darkness, light;
where there is sadness, joy.

O, divine Master, grant that I may not so much
seek to be consoled as to console;
to be understood as to understand;
to be loved, as to love;
for it is in giving that we receive;
it is in pardoning that we are pardoned;
it is in dying that we are born to eternal life. Amen!

St. Francis of Assisi

A prayer: "Lord, I choose to believe that you hold my life and future. Your timing has always been good and right in my life. You know best. My days, my weeks, months and years are recorded in your book of life. You decide and I follow. Help me to take each day with joy and thankfulness, seeking to give you first place. I trust you to give me a future that does not fade away. Thank you. Amen!"

Bibliography

Here are some of the authors and the titles of the books I have read and have been of great inspiration and encouragement to me:

Bennett, R. (1982); *Emotionally free;* Kingsway Publication Ltd

Bennett, R. (1987); *Making Peace with Your Inner Child;* Kingsway Publication Ltd

Harris, Amy and Thomas (1986); *Staying OK;* Pan Books Ltd

Huggett, Joyce (1986); *Listening to God;* Hodder and Stoughton

Lloyd-Jones, D. Martyn (1965); *Faith on Trial (Psalm 73);* first published by Inter-Varsity Fellowship

Morris, Jean C. (1983); *A Tool for Christians;* The Department of Education of the Church of Scotland

Morris, Jean C, (1983); *A Tool for Christians Book Two;* The Department of Education of the Church of Scotland

Nouwen, Henri J. M. (1986); *In the House of The Lord;* Darton, Longman and Todd Ltd

Nouwen, Henri J. M. (1989) *Seeds of Hope;* Darton, Longman and Todd Ltd

Pytches, Mary (1990); *Yesterday's Child;* Hodder and Stoughton

Pytches, Mary (1991); *A Child No More;* Hodder and Stoughton

Pytches, Mary (1987); *Set My People Free;* Hodder and Stoughton

Seaman, David A. (1987); *Put Away Childish Things;* Scripture Press Foundation (UK) Ltd

Seaman, David A. (1986); *Healing of Memories;* Scripture Press Foundation (UK) Ltd

Sister Margaret M. CSMV (1987); *Jesus Man of Prayer;* Hodder and Stoughton

Paul Tournier (1962); *A Place for You;* SCM Press LTD

Paul Tournier (1962); *Escape from loneliness;* SCM Press LTD